BRAVE MEN
TO THE BATTLE
The Story of the Waldenses

By Virgil E. Robinson

TEACH Services, Inc.
P U B L I S H I N G
www.TEACHServices.com

Copyright © 2012 Virgil E. Robinson and TEACH Services, Inc.
ISBN-13: 978-1-57258-164-7 (Paperback)
ISBN-13: 978-1-57258-921-6 (ePub)
ISBN-13: 978-1-57258-922-3 (Kindle/Mobi)

Library of Congress Control Number: 2011923670

Published by

TEACH Services, Inc.

P U B L I S H I N G

www.TEACHServices.com

Table of Contents

*For a thousand years the towering Alps helped protect
the Waldenses, a humble people who loved the Bible truths.*

1

A Place in the Wilderness

Amid the towering Alps of northwestern Italy, where the peaks point like fingers toward the skies, nestle fertile, grass-carpeted valleys. These valleys, which extend far into the heart of the lofty mountains, open into each other through narrow mountain passes. For a thousand years these valleys sheltered a humble people who wanted to be true to God without following the Church of Rome.

The valleys provided good homes for God's people. Torrents of water from snow-covered heights watered the land. The people grew food, raised sheep and cattle, and tended orchards and vineyards of sweet grapes. And because of their narrow entrances and the wall of mountains that enclosed them, the valleys proved to be magnificent natural fortresses that protected the people in times of trouble from their enemies. Many times a few men fighting behind barricades held off thousands of angry soldiers trying to enter the narrow passes.

The apostle John referred to these people several hundred years earlier when he wrote the last book of the Bible. In the twelfth chapter of Revelation he mentioned a beautiful woman facing a fierce dragon. The woman represented the true church of Jesus, while the dragon stood for Satan and his followers. John said the woman would flee from the dragon and find a place of refuge in the wilderness.

A man named Peter Waldo began preaching Bible truths about 1170. The priests called his beliefs heresy, which meant anything that disagreed with the teachings of the Roman Catholic Church. Many of the Christians in the Alpine valleys followed Waldo's teachings, and so they became known as Waldenses or another form of the word—*Vaudois* (pronounced voe-dwah).

For many years the Waldenses lived quietly in their mountain valleys, at peace with Catholic neighbors in the cities and towns of the plain. They had the Bible in their own language and completed handmade copies that they shared with others. Because the Waldenses feared that their precious Bible might sometime be taken from them, they memorized as much of it as they could. Even young children could repeat whole books of the Bible.

Priests from the nearby city of Turin sometimes visited the valleys trying to persuade the Vaudois to accept the teachings of the Roman Catholic Church and obey the laws of the pope, but they did not win many converts. The Waldensian pastors, called barbe, taught their flocks to be pure, kind, and friendly to all. They held the love of God in their hearts, and they wished to share with others the blessings they enjoyed.

The Waldenses believed it their duty to spread the true gospel of Jesus. They knew many people in the cities felt dissatisfied with the Catholic religion, but wandered in darkness seeking salvation. They met such people on the roads, making long pilgrimages to holy places. The priests had told them that by their works they could be saved. The Waldenses began making plans to carry the gospel to those poor people who had no Bible through which to learn the truth.

The Waldenses knew that Catholic leaders called them heretics because they did not obey the laws of the pope. They also knew that church leaders sometimes captured heretics and handed them over to the government to be burned at the stake. And so the Waldenses decided they would have to work quietly, according to Jesus' instruction to His disciples that they must be "wise as serpents, and harmless as doves."

They adopted a very simple plan. Young men went forth from their peaceful, sheltered valleys and traveled over much of Europe, not as missionaries, but as peddlers, carrying silks and satins, jewels, and fine silver plate for sale. When they came to a home where they suspected the family might welcome the gospel, they spoke cautiously of the plan of salvation. They often prayed in the homes, and before departing they usually left behind some portion of the Bible, one of the Gospels, perhaps the book of Psalms, or one of Paul's letters.

The Waldenses had another method of spreading their beliefs. Some of their most brilliant young men left their valley homes and went to the great schools in Paris, Milan, Bologna, Barcelona, or even Rome itself. In the universities they would mingle with the students, talking to them and asking questions. In this way they led many students to accept the teachings of the Waldenses.

When the Catholic Church leaders discovered the progress of the Waldenses, they became very angry. They commanded that the Waldenses be seized and put to death wherever found. They forbade the people to accept any portions of the Bible from the hands of visitors. They urged the university leaders not to allow the Waldenses to enter their schools.

"But," asked the schoolmasters, "how can we tell the Waldensian student from his fellows?"

"If you find someone who does not swear or gamble, drink or fight, he is probably a Waldensian."

Church authorities caught many of the Vaudois far from their home valleys. They usually gave the Vaudois the choice of renouncing their faith or being burned at the stake. Few would renounce their faith and enter the papal church, even to save their lives.

These victims were led outside the city walls, tied to a stake, and firewood heaped around them. Though they loved life, they would nevermore lift eyes to the lofty mountains of their homeland. But as they watched firewood being heaped around their feet, the words of Jesus came sweetly to their minds, giving strength, and sometimes even joy, in the hour of trial. They remembered the promise, "Be thou faithful unto death, and I will give thee a crown of life."

Did the Waldenses cease their missionary work because of such tragedies? No. Others came forward to take the places of those who had fallen. The pope in Rome grew angrier as he received reports from various parts of Europe telling of the work of the Waldenses. He decided that something had to be done. Not only must the Waldenses caught in the towns and cities be destroyed, but soldiers must go into their valleys and destroy the heretics completely. He summoned his cardinals and high church officers. They talked for a long time, planning how to bring the Waldenses back into the church and destroy all who would not submit.

2

Storm Clouds Gather

Across the Alps from the Waldenses lived a larger group of "heretics," the Albigenses. They occupied many flourishing towns and villages in southern France along the Rhone River. An industrious people, their ruler considered them among his best subjects.

A new man ascended the papal throne in 1198. He took the name Innocent III. He became the most powerful pope who ever ruled in Rome, and forced most of 'the kings and rulers of Europe to obey his commands. He severely punished those who did not. This pope called his church officers together to discuss how best to destroy the Albigenses and the Waldenses.

By this time the Waldenses had carried their doctrines to many parts of Europe. Small companies of people living in Naples, Poland, Germany, Moravia, Bohemia, and England worshiped God in the same way as the people in the valleys. But in France lived about two hundred thousand Albigenses. Innocent III decided to destroy them first.

He proclaimed a crusade, or holy war, against the Albigenses. In papal countries all over Europe the priests read the pope's proclamation. He invited all men to unite in an army to march against the Albigenses. He promised them the houses, lands, and goods of the heretics whom they killed. He also assured them that all soldiers killed in the crusade would have their sins forgiven and a sure place in heaven.

As a result, men from nearly every European country gathered in southern France and swelled into a mighty army. Much of the army, however, consisted of robbers, murderers, and adventurers who hoped to enrich themselves with the goods of the heretics.

The Albigenses had no soldiers, no strong forts, no way of defending themselves. They stood helpless while the horde of crusaders rolled over their beautiful country, stealing, killing, and burning. The army reduced the once flourishing country to a wasteland, and when the crusade ended, the Albigenses had been destroyed. Only a few managed to escape over the mountains and join the Waldenses.

A short time after the crusade, Pope Innocent III died, and the heretics settled into comparative peace.

More than a century later, John XXII became pope. He had read of Innocent III's crusade against the Albigenses, and sent two spies into the Waldensian valleys to investigate conditions there. The spies heard of a meeting attended by hundreds of Waldensian pastors and leaders. John quickly saw that the crusade of Innocent III had not destroyed all the heretics. But before he could complete the work, Pope John XXII died. The valleys remained in peace for another thirty years.

When Clement VI became pope, he wanted to see all of the Waldenses destroyed and their work in Europe brought to an end. He wrote to the kings of France and Naples, urging them to launch crusades against the Waldenses and their followers. He wrote a special letter to Johanna, wife of the king of Naples, urging her to help cleanse the valleys by destroying the heretics living there.

But the kings of France and Naples hesitated. The Waldenses were among their best citizens. They were prosperous, paid taxes promptly, and did not make trouble for their rulers. Why should the kings destroy such valuable citizens? So the rulers of Europe quietly ignored the instructions from the pope, and the Waldenses increased in numbers as the years of peace passed by.

Then came evil years for the papacy itself. A Frenchman who became pope moved the court from Rome to a French city, Avignon.

About seventy years passed before another pope, Gregory XI, returned the papacy from Avignon to Rome. Gregory died a year later, and the newly elected pope made the cardinals who had elected him angry. Thus they elected a second pope, who soon settled back in Avignon.

The French pope, of course, declared that he was the only true pope, and cursed the one in Rome. The Roman pope announced that he was the only true pope, and cursed the one in France. Many people didn't know which one to follow. A third pope was elected in 1409 to replace the other two popes, but neither of them would resign. Now three popes claimed supreme power, each cursing the others. Not until 1414 did one man regain complete control of the papacy.

So for a hundred years the Waldensian valleys lay more or less in peace, as none of the popes had time to bother them.

Actually persecution never stopped completely, The Roman Church sent men called inquisitors to search out all who did not worship in the papal way, that they might be put to death. In the year 1400, one of these inquisitors assembled some soldiers and led them into one of the Waldensian valleys. They completely surprised the poor Waldenses. The inquisitors captured one hundred and fifty men plus several women and children, and took them to Grenoble where they put them to death.

Elated with this successful first effort, the inquisitor, Borelli, decided to repeat it. This time he knew the Waldenses would be watchful, so he waited until midwinter, when snow blocked the passes.

Then with his soldiers he entered the valley and marched on the little town of Pragelas. Someone saw them coming, a long line of black figures against the pure-white snow, and he shouted an alarm to the village. Parents picked up their children, young men carried the old people and the sick. The shades of a long winter night fell as the soldiers came to the village and, following the fresh tracks in the snow, quickly caught up with the fleeing procession. They killed many of the weak and helpless, spilling red blood on the white snow, Then, as darkness fell, the soldiers returned to the village and spent the night in the abandoned homes of its people.

The villagers had no rest that dreadful night. They tried to cross the mountain pass to San Martin, another Waldensian valley, but in the darkness and storm many lost their way. Some fell from high cliffs. Others sank in the snow and never rose again. The morning light revealed a terrible sight. Many of the Waldenses had frozen hands and feet. Some carried children who had died during the night. The people found fifty young children dead in the arms of mothers who had fallen in the deep snow beside the path.

This great tragedy took place on Christmas Eve, and even to this day fathers and mothers in Pragelas tell their children of the saddest Christmas ever known in their valley.

Although the Waldenses suffered much during these persecutions, they still survived. When church or state authorities captured their missionaries in France, England, Germany, or Italy, and put them to death, other youth gladly took their places. Finally many church authorities decided that the Waldensian missionaries must be stopped and that the only way to stop them was to destroy the whole Waldensian nation.

In 1487, Pope Innocent VIII reigned in Rome. He remembered how a former pope who bore the same name had destroyed the Albigenses of France. He wanted to become as famous as his predecessor, so he issued a long statement about Waldenses, declaring them the worst heretics in the world. He demanded that they all be killed.

"If they do not give up their faith," declared the thoroughly angry pope, "let them be crushed like poisonous snakes."

He began by searching for a man to organize a crusade. He chose Cataneo, a famous Italian captain. Then the pope wrote to the king of France and to Charles II, the duke of Savoy, commanding them to send armies to help Cataneo destroy the heretics. He urged all Catholic church members to come to the help of Cataneo. Once again an army gathered to exterminate heretics, and again the pope promised the soldiers that they could keep all the goods of the heretics they killed.

In Turin, Cataneo sat down with his other officers and laid his plans. One company would assemble in France and attack the Waldenses from that side, while he would advance with his army from the Italian side. By attack from both sides at once, he expected to destroy the Waldenses completely and to crush their faith forever.

The Waldenses attacked the 700 invaders and destroyed them.
Only one was left to flee up the mountain in the darkness.

3

Trapped in a Cave

A cruel but daring captain named La Palu led the soldiers who advanced against the Waldenses from the French side of the Alps. He and his men first attacked the people living in the Vallouise. Some herders far up on the mountainside saw them coming and ran swiftly to the village to warn the people. The Waldenses watched their enemies coming over the mountain pass, and knew that La Palu had twenty times as many soldiers in his army as they could send against him. They could do nothing but flee. Putting their old men, women, and children into carts with stores of food, and driving their flocks of goats, sheep, and cattle before them, they began to ascend the steep slopes of Mount Peloux. They sang psalms of David as they climbed higher and higher above the valley floor. The summit towered above them. The mountain canyons echoed with the sound of their voices.

Some of the old and feeble fell behind. The soldiers hastened after them, killing the stragglers. But the majority of the company reached a well-known cave on the mountainside. Into this cave they fled with their animals. The women and children hurried far back into the gloomy depths of the cavern while the men stood at the mouth, ready to resist any attempt of the soldiers to force an entrance. They had piles of large stones ready to roll down on the heads of anyone trying to climb to the cave.

La Palu saw the danger and knew it would be fatal to lead his men, untrained in this type of warfare, under the ledge of the cave. Instead he guided them around the side of the mountain and climbed it from the rear. He then took them to a point directly over the mouth of the cave. Using ropes brought with them for hanging the Waldenses, the soldiers lowered some of their number onto the platform in front of the cave.

The Waldenses had not anticipated an attack from above, and seemed paralyzed with fright as they watched their enemies. It would have been easy to kill that first small group of soldiers, but these people had lived so long in peace that the thought of fighting, even for their lives, seemed foreign to them.

Since their enemies had captured the mouth of the cave, the Waldenses retired far back into the gloomy interior rooms along well-known paths. La Palu's soldiers dared not enter the heart of the cave without a guide. The captain, realizing the danger that would come to his men in that strange, dark place, ordered his soldiers to gather large piles of brush from the mountainside. They heaped these high at the mouth of the cavern, and set them on fire. Silently, down into the deep interior of the cave rolled great billows of smoke. The Waldenses had no way of escape and died from suffocation.

Altogether three thousand people perished in that cave. The army had destroyed the entire population of Vallouise, and the Waldenses never again occupied that beautiful valley.

La Palu then led his army into another valley, killing the people and destroying their homes. As word of his coming went before him, many of the people fled over the passes into more protected valleys. Still so many of the Vaudois lost their lives that the soldiers of La Palu soon found they could not carry all the loot they collected from the homes of their victims. Naturally the soldiers hoped that such a profitable war would continue for a long time.

The last valley La Palu entered was Pragelas, the community which had been so terribly afflicted on Christmas Eve eighty-seven years before. The crusaders fell upon the village without warning. Many unsuspecting farmers fell in the fields while reaping their harvests. Others fled far up toward the tops of the mountains. Some of these, not having heard of the fate of the people in Vallouise, took refuge in caves, where La Palu repeated the tragedy. His soldiers kindled fires at the mouths of these caves and the people inside suffocated.

Not all the people of Pragelas died. After recovering from the shock of the sudden attack, they turned boldly on the invaders and attacked them. Most of the soldiers of La Palu's army had been brigands and robbers before joining the crusade, and did not know how to fight. When the Waldenses attacked, they fled in terror. Many of them died in the valley they had expected to conquer so easily.

Meanwhile on the Italian side of the Alps the papal legate, Cataneo, led his army across the plains of Piedmont and into the foothills where he prepared for a war which he expected would wipe out every Waldensian settlement. The inhabitants of villages living near the plain, realizing that they could not successfully resist, fell back into their mountain fastnesses. The papal soldiers plundered their homes, then set them on fire.

Seeing little hope of resisting such a mighty host, the Waldenses sent two of their oldest and wisest men to plead with Cataneo. They protested that they only obeyed the Word of God, and offered to surrender any doctrine which the priests could prove contrary to what the Bible taught. Because they spoke meekly, Cataneo thought they must be a weak people. So he mocked them and sent them back with fearful threats of what would happen unless they submitted.

Thinking that he would not need to use his whole army against such a peaceful and unwarlike people, he divided it into two separate bands, intending to send each group into a different valley. But he was to discover that the Waldenses were not so weak as they appeared.

Cataneo's army marched until it came to the town of La Torre. They found it deserted, the people having fled into the more inaccessible valleys. Along the road beside the beautiful river of Pelice the papal soldiers continued their journey, passing through Villaro and other villages as they ascended the valley of Lucerna. At the head of this valley they came to the town of Bobbio which they captured easily, for its inhabitants had also fled over the mountains. Because Cataneo's men had met with no opposition, they began to consider themselves very good soldiers.

While one regiment advanced into the valley of Lucerna, the other turned in another direction in order to destroy the heretics in the valley of Angrogna, the heart of the Waldenses' country. If this valley fell, all hope of preserving the people would be gone.

Meanwhile the soldiers who had taken Bobbio so easily decided to climb over the mountain pass into Prali, kill its inhabitants, then go on to the valleys of San Martin and Perosa. From there they would march into Angrogna and rejoin the other branch of the army. The war would be over, and the mountains free of heretics. They felt sure the pope would be pleased and give them his blessing.

One morning seven hundred soldiers marched out of Bobbio toward Prali. As the men climbed higher on the steep path they could see the village from which they had come far below. With their weapons in their hands, and wearing heavy armor, they soon grew tired of the climb. Frequently they stopped to rest or to refresh themselves by drinking from the mountain streams which crossed their path. Above them towered the mighty Alpine peaks, but these men had no time to look upon the beauties of God's creation. They thought only of the village they would soon attack, the people they would kill, and the booty they would collect.

Finally they reached the top of the pass. Glad to be finished with the long climb, they began their descent, certain of sure victory in the village.

But Cataneo's soldiers could not know that the sharp eyes of a village boy far below had seen them coming over the top of the pass, and that he had spread the alarm throughout the valley. Men left their work and came hurrying from all directions. Some carried swords, some axes, some scythes, and some had only slings; but all had stout hearts, strong arms, and an abiding faith in God. They well knew that their lives as well as those of their women and children depended on bold action that day. Could they defeat the army slowly coming down the mountain toward them?

Cataneo's soldiers found the descent of three thousand feet almost as tiring as the climb had been. When they finally reached the valley floor, they were widely scattered. Then, coming through the woods, they beheld the embattled Waldenses drawn up across their path, prepared to fight for their homes.

Raising a feeble shout the weary papal soldiers rushed toward their foes, but all in vain. The Waldenses not only defeated the invaders but destroyed them. Of the seven hundred men who had climbed the mountain and descended on Prali, only one fled back up the mountain in the gathering darkness. There, in a crevice behind a snow bank, be hid for several days until hunger and cold finally drove him out. Then he humbly entered the village of Prali to throw himself on the mercy of the men he had come to kill.

Satisfied with their victory, the Waldenses cared for the fugitive, then sent him back across the mountain pass to report to the commander in Bobbio that he alone of the seven hundred soldiers had escaped the swords of the Waldenses.

4

God Sends a Cloud

When the Waldenses realized that Cataneo and his soldiers really meant to destroy them, they decided to battle for their lives and their faith. They knew that they could never face an army on any open battlefield. Being simple farmers, they possessed few weapons. So they began a great withdrawal into the inner fastnesses of their mountains. Thousands, old and young, with flocks and herds left the smiling fields in the foothills and journeyed into the inner valleys of Lucerna, San Martin, and especially Angrogna.

Scouts told Cataneo of this movement, and the news pleased him. In this way, he thought, all his enemies would be concentrated in two or three places, and could be destroyed at one time. News had not yet reached the captain of the total defeat of his detachments in the valley of Lucerna.

Meanwhile the Waldenses busied themselves preparing all the weapons they knew how to make. A few owned swords. Quite a number armed themselves with bows and arrows. As Cataneo's army entered the lower end of the valley of Angrogna and pushed along the narrow road beside the stream, they soon came to the principal company of Waldenses. The Waldenses had put up a rude barricade of logs across the road. Directly behind the barricade stood the men, manning the defenses. In the rear old people, women, and children gathered in a hollow for protection.

Rejoicing at the opportunity to use their swords against people they had been led to despise, the papal forces shouted and rushed forward to overthrow that thin line behind the barricade. They discharged a shower of arrows, and for a moment it seemed that the Waldensian line would fall. The women and children, who watched with trembling hearts, fell on their knees, stretched their arms toward heaven, and cried out, "O God of our fathers, help us! Help us!"

The papal soldiers heard their cry and raised another shout, anticipating immediate victory. One of them, Captain Le Noir, a proud, headstrong man, stepped forward, calling the Waldenses cowards.

"Pray on!" he shouted, "and see how much good it does you." Pushing back his heavy brass helmet he continued in a mocking tone, "Nothing can save you now!"

He had scarcely uttered the words when a powerful arrow, shot from the bow of Pierre Revel, struck him and pierced his forehead between the eyes. He fell dead.

With a shout the Waldenses all along the line rushed forward. The papal soldiers, disheartened by the loss of their champion, began to fall back. The Waldenses chased them clear out of the valley, and that evening camped once again at the entrance to Angrogna.

This failure dismayed and angered Cataneo. The next day be set his army in motion again, pushing up the same road until they came to the place of their defeat the day before. To their surprise, they found no one there. They advanced steadily, watching carefully lest they fall into an ambush, but they could not see anybody.

Pushing on up the valley which gradually became narrower, they discovered a narrow pass, washed out through the years by ice cold waters of the Angrogna stream. A path led through this gorge, a path so narrow that not more than two men could walk side by side. High above the waters, that path would doubtless lead them into the inner valley, where they expected to find the Waldenses camping around their headquarters at Pra Del Tor. Cataneo felt sure that if he could follow them, he would be able to destroy them all and end the campaign victoriously.

He boldly ordered his army forward into the pass, a truly fearful place. Sometimes the dense foliage of the trees hid the waters of the river from view. The mountainside rose steeply to the right of the path three thousand feet into the sky. Along the path marched Cataneo's army, two by two in a long narrow line.

The Waldenses had been watching every movement of their foes. Scouts on the mountainsides had signaled the enemy's entrance into the gorge. They posted a strong guard at the place where the path widened out into the valley in which they had taken refuge. They had a strong faith in God and they believed that He would protect them. just how He would do it, they did not know. Perhaps He would shake the earth and send the mountains crashing down on the heads of their enemies. Perhaps He would rain hailstones out of heaven on them. Or perhaps the angel of the Lord might smite them as he had smitten Sennacherib's host.

Looking up, they noticed thick dark clouds gathering on the tops of the mountain peaks overlooking the valley. As they watched, fascinated, those clouds began to creep down the mountainside, lower and lower. Had God chosen the clouds to save them? Down, down came the clouds, finally rolling into the chasm where the soldiers toiled up the path, sealing it from top to bottom and shutting out the light of day.

Astonished at the gloom which had suddenly fallen upon them, the papal soldiers stood still, not daring to move forward or backward. The Waldenses raised a loud shout. They climbed the hills above the gorge and began to roll tremendous rocks down into the canyon. The great rocks crushed dozens of papal soldiers where they stood. Panic overwhelmed them. They tried to flee, but in the darkness missed their way. Many fell over the edge and into the stream far below. Few of those who had so confidently entered the chasm in bright sunlight a few hours before got back to tell Cataneo of their failure.

Discouraged by this second defeat, Cataneo fell back with his army to La Torre. While waiting there, wondering how to report his failure to the duke of Savoy, he received a report of the complete defeat of the detachments he had sent into the valleys of Lucerne and Prali. Filled with a superstitious dread that perhaps he might fall beneath the swords of these mountain farmers too, he went down onto the plain of Piedmont to establish new headquarters.

From this new point, Cataneo sent small flying detachments of men into various parts of the valleys, continuing these harassing tactics for a year. The soldiers surprised many Waldenses, cutting them off far from their homes. They burned the homes of the Waldenses and drove away their cattle, sheep, and goats. But the invaders had even heavier losses. The Waldenses posted scouts at various points to keep close watch over the movements of their enemies. Flying squads of mountaineers formed to cut off the soldiers Cataneo sent into the valleys.

Through it all, the Waldenses continued to pray for peace in order that they might return to their homes and work without fear of these sudden attacks. Finally, the duke of Savoy decided to stop the persecutions. He sent an envoy into the valleys, inviting the people whom he had failed to conquer to send representatives to a peace conference.

Twelve of their wisest men traveled to Turin where they talked with the duke. He asked them many curious questions about their religious beliefs, and they explained their faith, showing how they simply tried to follow the Bible.

The duke could see that he had been told many lies about the Waldenses. To these representatives he expressed his deep regret for the losses they had endured. He had not known what they really did believe. Before the envoys returned to the valleys, the duke made a solemn promise that the persecutions would stop. At the same time, he made a strange request.

"Would it be possible for me to see twelve of your small children?"

The Waldensian men looked at one another in astonishment, wondering why the prince wanted to see their children. Then they agreed to send for them. A few weeks later, twelve mothers escorted their small children into the presence of the prince. He looked at the children carefully, and seemed surprised by what he saw. The Waldenses became more puzzled than ever.

"What is it that surprises your excellency?" they asked.

"These children seem to be quite normal. Do you know what I was told?"

"No, sir. We have no idea."

"The priests told me that Waldensian children were born with only one eye in the middle of the forehead, and that they also had four rows of black teeth."

The envoys smiled, pointing to their happy, healthy children. The prince could see that the priests had lied to him.

With the promise from their prince that they would not be disturbed again on account of religion, the Waldenses returned to their valleys. For fifty years no further attempts were made to destroy the Waldensian people.

5

A New Light in Europe

The war had ended. From places of refuge among the mountains, in caves, or in thick forests, the Waldenses returned to their homes. They had much work to do, rebuilding burned homes and planting new trees and crops to replace the ones destroyed. Many families would never be the same again. Fathers and brothers had been killed in battle. Mothers had been struck down as they fled from their homes. Many children had been carried away, never to be seen again, placed in Catholic schools among the cities of the plain.

Sadly the Waldenses looked at their ruined churches. Hardly one had escaped the torch of the invader. But in spite of all their troubles the Waldenses felt thankful that their tiny nation had survived when it seemed it would be totally destroyed. Under the shadows of the lofty peaks, under the blue dome of heaven, the pastors could again hold mass meetings. The people sang songs and offered prayers of thanks to God for sparing them.

About one question, however, the Waldenses held divided opinions. Should they rebuild their ruined churches? The pastors and older members of the community thought they should, but the younger people did not think it wise.

"As soon as we rebuild our churches," they said, "the papists will see them and become angry, and will launch another war against us. It would be better for us to worship in our homes and hold general meetings in the forests where our enemies will not see us. Then they will leave us in peace." Reluctantly the older people agreed to try this plan.

Now that the war had been called off, the Waldenses remained safe so long as they remained in their valleys. With this peace and safety, however, came another problem. Now that they no longer had to fight for their religion, many lost sight of their faith. They did not meet regularly for church services and in some valleys they did not meet at all. Even their former zeal to take the gospel to other parts of Europe disappeared. Although some still traveled to other countries, they avoided doing anything to arouse the anger of the church authorities. They had suffered terribly and had no desire to stir up the anger of their enemies again.

Some Waldenses went even further in trying to conceal their religion. Knowing they could not travel safely as known Waldenses they went to the priests and asked for a paper that said they were good Catholics and should not be molested. The priests cooperated on condition that they attend the Roman church and have their children baptized into that faith. Many Waldenses, thinking to secure peace for themselves and their families, did as the priests requested. After all, they reasoned, the priests need never know what they taught their children at home.

As the older men and women saw the faith and zeal of their people growing weaker, they became very sad. They did what they could to encourage everyone to stand up for the faith they had received from their fathers, the faith for which so many had died. No longer, however, did the children memorize long passages from the Bible, and it became increasingly difficult to find young men willing to accept the hard and often dangerous life of a pastor.

Then, Waldenses who had been traveling in foreign lands returned to their home valleys with strange and exciting news. In Germany, in Switzerland, and in France, they had found Christians who no longer went to mass, who did not obey the pope, or attend his church. These people had the Bible, and believed that through faith in Jesus they would be saved. They prayed to God and refused to confess their sins to any priest. They did not bow down to images or go on long pilgrimages.

This news thrilled the people of the valleys. Everyone asked questions. Where had these Christians found a religion so much like theirs?

Of course, though these travelers didn't realize it, they had seen beginnings of the great Reformation started by Martin Luther, Melanchthon, Zwingli, and others. The similarities between the beliefs of the Protestants, as these people came to be called, and Waldensian beliefs surprised the people of the valleys. News of the Waldenses likewise surprised the Protestants, Some of the Protestant leaders visited the Waldensian valleys to study and compare the two religious faiths.

When the Protestant ministers came, they felt both pleased and saddened. As they talked with the Waldensian pastors, they found to their joy that the Waldenses rejected the teachings of the papal church, and that they taught the same things from the Bible as the Protestants. But the Protestants also felt sad because the religious faith of the mountain people had grown dim. They urged that the ruined churches be rebuilt. They also advised the Waldenses to stop attending services in the Roman church, even for the sake of peace.

The Waldenses, shamed that these new followers of their faith should have to rebuke them, quickly set to work rebuilding their churches. They stopped attending Catholic services and allowing their children to be baptized by the priests.

"Let us call a council of all Christians who believe the Bible and refuse to obey the pope," urged some of the pastors. Messengers traveled to Switzerland, Germany, France, and Italy, inviting Protestants in those lands to send delegates.

In October, 1532, the assembly met in Chamforans, a settlement in the valley of Angrogna, the heart of the Waldensian territory. For six days the meetings continued, and when they closed, the leaders had drawn up a statement showing that the Waldenses and the Protestants shared the same truths.

"What can we do for our brethren in Switzerland and France?" asked the Waldenses. "What can we give that will prove of most value to them?" After much discussion they voted to have the Bible translated and printed in the French language. The Waldenses, none of whom were wealthy, collected 1,500 gold crowns. They asked a man by the name of Olivetan to do the translating work. His cousin, the famous Protestant scholar, John Calvin, helped him. In 1535 a French Bible was printed. It proved a great blessing to French-speaking Protestants everywhere. In this way the ancient church of the Alps repaid its debt to the Protestants who had done so much to help rekindle religious faith in the heart of the Waldensian valleys.

During the next twenty-eight years, terrible persecution befell the Waldenses. In 1537, priests persuaded the duke of Savoy who ruled the Piedmont plain and those parts of the Alps where the Waldenses lived, that to save his soul, he must destroy the heretics. The duke consented. He directed a nobleman named Bersour to collect an army, then to conquer and destroy all Waldenses who refused to return to the Catholic Church.

Bersour quickly made ready to obey his order. With five hundred horsemen and soldiers he advanced boldly into the valleys, directing his attack mainly on the valley of Angrogna. But the Waldenses drove him back and chased him out of the country. Furious, he attacked Waldenses who had been living in peace on the plains around Turin and threw hundreds of them into prison.

Many were burned in the months that followed, among them, Catalan Girard. Even while being tied to the stake, with wood piled around him, he thought only of those nearby who knew not Christ.

"Bring me two stones," he cried out, shortly before time to kindle the fire at his feet. Someone brought two stones. Taking them in his hands, he held them up high and began to rub them together.

"You think you can extinguish our churches by your persecutions. You can no more do so than I, with my feeble hands, can crush these stones." Then as the flames leaped around him, he sang hymns as long as he could.

The Waldenses in the valleys heard of these martyrdoms. Did this mean, they asked fearfully, that the persecutions of the past which had not troubled them for many years, had returned to trouble them now? Many people related stories their parents had told them of fearful times in the past. They recalled what the church had endured when Cataneo and his bands of ruffians devastated their valleys. Would they see such dreadful days again? They began to pray and seek God, pleading that in His mercy He would save His people.

God answered their prayers but perhaps not in the manner they had expected. The king of France wished to invade Italy. To do so, he must lead his army through the Alps. The best route would take him through the passes held by the Waldenses. So he sent a request to the duke for permission to pass through the valleys of the Waldenses.

The duke of Savoy, not wishing to see the French in Italy, refused this request. Then he remembered that those passes lay in the bands of the Waldenses, the people he was persecuting and trying to destroy. He immediately decided to make peace with his faithful subjects, lest they open the passes and let the French through. He sent word to Bersour to stop all attacks on the Waldenses. He even set free those still in prison, and they returned home rejoicing.

But the French king entered Italy by another route. The war continued for several years. When peace finally returned, the valleys became part of the dominion of France. During the next three centuries, those valleys passed back and forth between France and Piedmont several times.

Although direct attacks on the valleys stopped for nearly twenty years, persecution of Waldenses still continued outside the valleys. One of their most learned pastors, Martin Conon, went to the city of Geneva to talk with John Calvin. On his way back, he passed through Dauphine where authorities arrested him and charged him with being a spy. He proved that this was not true. However, among his papers his captors found evidence that he was something far worse in their eyes, a heretic. They immediately condemned him to death. They would have liked to burn him at the stake, but greatly feared the effect his dying words might have on the bystanders. So in the middle of the night they led him from his dungeon and took him to the Isere River, where they drowned him.

Those captured and put to death included one man who made a deep impression on his captors. Barthelemy Hector, a humble bookseller, fell into the hands of a priest, who dragged him to Turin and there accused him of selling heretical books.

"You have been caught in the act of selling books that contain heresy," said the judge. "What do you have to say?"

"If the Bible is heresy to you, it is truth to me."

"But you use the Bible to stop men from going to mass."

"If the Bible stops men from going to mass, it is proof that God does not approve of it, and that mass is idolatry."

The judge could not endure this kind of talk. Leaning forward, pointing his finger at the prisoner, he shouted, "Retract!"

"I have spoken only truth," replied the brave bookseller. "Can I change truth as I would a garment?"

For several months his judges kept Barthelemy in prison, hoping that he would recant. The priests feared that burning Waldenses only made people more willing to accept the faith of the heretics, so they hesitated to burn them publicly. But in the end, they brought Barthelemy before a large crowd of people and burned him at the stake.

In 1559, the valleys returned to the possession of the duke of Savoy. At that time, the king of France and the duke signed a treaty, one term of which demanded that the duke of Savoy destroy all heretics. A tempest, blacker and more terrible than any they had thus far endured, broke over the heads of the Waldenses.

*The Waldensian clasped his attacker by the knees
and hurled himself from the precipice, so that they fell together.*

6

A Threat From Savoy

One ominous day, the duke of Savoy sent messengers galloping on horseback into every town and village of his territories, including the Waldensian valleys. The Waldensian people trembled as they arrived, for already rumors flew in regard to serious trouble ahead. On the notice boards in towns and village squares the messengers posted proclamations signed by the duke. With anxious faces and pounding hearts, the people assembled to read the duke's message. Usually they chose one man to read the proclamation aloud. After the reading the people looked at one another in dismay. Could it be possible? Had they heard right? The reader repeated it, item by item.

Any person, anywhere in the territory of the duke of Savoy, who went to hear the Protestant preachers, would be fined one hundred pieces of gold for the first offense, the notice said. If caught a second time, they would be sent to the galleys, to spend the rest of their lives as slaves.

The Waldenses got little sleep that night. Nor did they get much work done during the following days. They could not understand how their ruler could publish such a cruel edict. He had always seemed such a kind man, and he had a Protestant wife.

They did not know, however, that messengers had arrived at the duke's court from the pope and the kings of France and Spain, three of the most powerful rulers of Europe, warning Emmanuel Philbert that if he did not destroy the heretics in his kingdom, they would send their armies and do it for him. If this happened he would never rule the valleys again, they warned him.

Hoping that they might be able to change the edict, the Waldenses selected two leaders to deliver a protest at the duke's court. Very humbly they pleaded that their people not be condemned without an opportunity to speak in self-defense. They had always paid their taxes faithfully. Crime did not exist in the mountain valleys. No Vaudois criminals languished in the duke's prisons. Never had they molested their Catholic neighbors. They warned the duke that if he shed their blood, it would cry to God for vengeance like the blood of Abel, and the curse of Cain would come on his house. The duchess, who sympathized with the Waldenses, added her tears and pleas to those of the ambassadors. The duke dismissed his visitors and promised to reconsider the matter. The edicts would remain suspended until further word came to the Waldenses.

The duke would gladly have spared the lives of these peaceful and obedient subjects. But the Catholic rulers of Europe urged him to get on with the task of their destruction, and he dared not refuse. Still he waited for three months, hoping that some miracle would enable him to spare them. The Waldenses waited for further word also, hoping that the decree might be reversed. But their enemies could not restrain their eagerness. Bands of ruffians began attacking the mountain villages, killing the people and seizing their goods. At first the Vaudois did not fight back. Surely, they thought, open war would be better than this.

In an effort to gain more time, the duke sent his brother, Philip of Savoy, into the valleys to try to persuade the people to return to the church of Rome. A kindly man, Philip listened to a sermon by one of the "heretics" and found it good doctrine, He then invited the people to listen to some priests he had brought with him, and they agreed. But the priests could not show from the Bible that the Waldenses were wrong, so they made no converts. Discouraged, Philip reported to the duke his lack of success. The ambassadors from France and Spain and the pope became more demanding than ever.

"There is only one way to destroy heresy, and that is to attack the people with fire and sword," they urged. "They will never listen to the priests."

Reluctantly the duke drew up another edict in which he declared war on the Waldenses. In order to make the campaign short, he sent word throughout Italy inviting all men to join his army and help conquer the Waldenses. Ruffians, brigands, thieves, and criminals of all sorts joined regular soldiers in preparing to invade the homeland of the Vaudois.

The pope offered large rewards to all who joined this crusade. As Pope Innocent III had done in the crusade against the Albigenses, this pope promised that if anyone died fighting the heretics, his sins would be forgiven and he would be sure of salvation. The soldiers also knew that if successful in fighting they could plunder the towns and villages of the Waldenses, seizing whatever they wanted.

The count La Trinita, a cruel and blood-thirsty man, took command of the first group of 4,000 men and boldly advanced into the mountains.

With the enemy at the gates, the Waldenses humbled themselves, fasted and prayed. Together they partook of the Lord's Supper. Then they sent their old men and women, their wives and little children deep into the inner valleys, while they prepared to halt the advancing army of enemies. Although the total population of the valleys at this time numbered about eighteen thousand, it included only about fifteen hundred fighting men.

The Piedmontese army entered the lower end of the valley of Angrogna and spread themselves out in battle array. A small group of the Vaudois stood their ground and fought manfully to prevent the enemy from advancing farther into the valley. All afternoon they battled, but the Vaudois could not drive back the much larger army. Very few of the mountain men had swords. Most of them fought with bows and arrows, while some had only sling-shots.

When the sun went down, neither side had gained a victory, but the Waldenses had been pushed back up the valley. Casting aside their weapons, the soldiers on both sides lighted camp fires and prepared their evening meal.

Suddenly a shout of laughter from the Piedmontese soldiers broke the evening calm. On the summit of a nearby hill, they had seen the figures of the Waldenses outlined against the sky, kneeling with arms outstretched to heaven, and praying to God for help. But yet another sound interrupted the soldiers' laughter. From somewhere in the darkness they heard the steady beating of a drum. It seemed to come nearer and nearer.

"That's another army coming to help the Vaudois!" exclaimed a captain. The idea of being attacked by superior forces, especially in darkness, filled the soldiers with terror. Panic seized them.

Hundreds of men turned and fled from the battlefield, casting away their arms as they ran. They lost all the ground which had been gained that day, and did not stop until they were several miles down the valley. Some Waldenses, meanwhile, rolled rocks down on the fleeing soldiers. The next morning the Waldenses collected the weapons which the invaders had so hastily thrown aside. Count La Trinita had lost sixty-seven men, while only three of the Vaudois had fallen.

The Waldenses, as startled by the sound of the drum as their enemies, were eager to know who had beaten it. An investigation revealed that a little child had found an old drum and started beating it just for fun. In such a simple way God answered the prayers of his helpless followers.

In a great rage over what had happened, La Trinita led his army into the exposed Waldensian towns outside the mountain valleys. There his soldiers burned and pillaged without mercy. They killed only a few, however, for most of the people had already withdrawn deep into the mountains. Three more times La Trinita tried to enter the valley of Angrogna with his army, and three times the Waldenses drove him back with great loss.

La Trinita finally realized he would have much difficulty conquering these hardy mountaineers. Perhaps it might be easier to subdue the heretics in some other way. He knew the Vaudois were completely truthful, and no doubt would expect other men to be like themselves. So he sent messengers under a flag of truce to the Vaudois camp bearing the message that he wished to make peace. Always happy to stop fighting, some of the mountaineers entered the camp of the count.

He first flattered them, saying how brave they had been and what good soldiers they made. Then he said it was evident that the pope had been misinformed about them, for apparently they were not heretics. If they wanted peace, they would need to do only a few things.

"What are your requirements? asked the cautious Waldensian envoys.

"Just allow some priests to go through your valleys and enter your churches and say mass there."

The Waldenses thought this might be possible, After all, they could purify their churches again after the priests departed. They discussed the matter with their people. The pastors urged them to make no concessions, but the people, eager for peace, agreed, Priests traveled through the valleys, but the armies did not withdraw.

"What more must we do?" asked the anxious Waldenses.

"You must lay down your arms, and let me establish garrisons in your villages to help keep the peace. At the same time you should send deputies to the duke and ask him for terms of peace."

The Waldenses discussed this, Again the pastors urged against it, but again the people decided to trust the word of the count. But the count's soldiers continued plundering and killing the Waldenses. For the third time their envoys entered his camp.

"What more must we do?"

"You must send away every one of your pastors. This is my last demand. If you will do this, then the war is over."

With great sadness the Vaudois sent their pastors away. The winter snow lay deep in the mountain passes as the poor men struggled up over the mountains and down into Pragelas, a French Protestant village.

La Trinita now had the people fully in his power. With their pastors gone, their spirits seemed completely broken. Papal soldiers occupied the valleys, burning, plundering and killing the people. The soldiers hunted the people through the forests, shooting them down as they would wild animals.

They followed one old man far up the side of the mountain. A Piedmontese soldier gradually crowded him back onto the edge of a cliff. Thinking he would enjoy watching the man fall, he rushed at the old man to hurl him over. But in this soldier, the Waldensian saw an enemy of his people. Clasping his attacker by the knees, he hurled himself over the edge, carrying the soldier with him to death hundreds of feet below.

The destruction continued. The army drove off cattle, sheep and goats. They smashed to pieces the mills with which the people ground their wheat. They cut down fruit trees and filled wells with stones. The count evidently intended to starve the people to death. By deceit he accomplished much more than he ever could have done with his soldiers.

The last blow came when the deputies returned from the duke. The Waldenses in the valley of Angrogna gathered to hear the message from their prince. But even before the deputies spoke, the people knew from their sorrowful faces that they had failed.

With groans and sobs they told the people the dreadful news. The house of Savoy refused to make peace. The Waldenses had their decision, either return to the church of Rome, or be utterly exterminated. The duke had begun to raise another large army to finish the work that La Trinita's men had begun.

The stunned people desperately needed the wise advice of their pastors now. They realized how greatly they had been deceived by La Trinita.

Although they knew what the answer would be, the deputies asked the question, "Are you willing to go to mass and return to the Church of Rome?"

With hands uplifted to heaven, the people sent back the reply. Their defiant words echoed through the mountain valleys:

"No! No! Never!"

7

The Answer From the Alps

Before many days passed Waldenses in even the most remote villages heard of the dreadful choice the duke of Savoy offered them. As church bells rang out the alarm, men and women left their work, and gathered in village squares to discuss the matter. Solemnly the older men put the question to the people.

"Are you willing to surrender your churches to the priests, to accept their teachings, and renounce the faith we have received from our fathers?"

"Impossible!" cried the people. Yet if they did not surrender, what future lay before them and their children? The duke had plainly stated that he would exterminate the Waldenses and give their valleys to another people if they did not yield.

In that black hour of despair the people naturally thought with longing of their beloved pastors. But those good men now lived in Pragelas, on the other side of the lofty, snow-blocked Alps. Someone suggested that they be invited to return.

"Do you think they will come?" the younger men asked. "Think how badly we treated them. We refused to listen when they warned us against accepting La Trinita's terms."

"Of course they will return," the elders reassured them. "They would lay down their lives for us, if necessary."

"Then let us send for them immediately. If we must die, let us all perish together. They will bring the blessing of God with them. Who knows whether God may not work for us and deliver us as He did our fathers."

So messengers traveled over the mountains. The pastors did not hesitate in answering the call from their people. Back over the mountains they followed the messengers and once again took charge of the villages.

"This is your opportunity to show the world that you are true men," they urged. "Remember, we serve the powerful God of heaven, who will just as willingly help His people now as He did the Israelites by the Red Sea."

No longer did the people talk of surrender. The pastors called for a great general meeting. Since all the people could not fit into a meetinghouse, they met in the forest. Here they pledged to fight unitedly for their homes and their faith.

First they cleansed the churches which had been used for months by the priests La Trinita had scattered throughout the valleys. They destroyed every image, picture, and candle. Then the pastors entered and preached the Word of God to the people.

They spent weekdays preparing for the great struggle which lay ahead. All day and often far into the night the people worked. Every house became a factory where they made muskets, bullets, swords, pikes, and even bows and arrows. They erected barricades along the mountain trails which would delay any army seeking to enter the valleys.

One company of Waldenses went down into the valley to cleanse the temple at Villaro. On the way they met the first band of La Trinita's soldiers, marching into the valley to receive the surrender of the heretics. A brief, sharp fight followed, and the Waldenses defeated the soldiers, who fled back to Villaro. The Waldenses followed and besieged them. In vain La Trinita sent three bands of soldiers to rescue his men. On the tenth day of the siege, the soldiers surrendered. The Vaudois spared their lives and escorted them to La Torre.

La Trinita felt enraged when he heard of the loss of Villaro, and he determined to launch a strong campaign. But first he tried his old trick, sending emissaries who offered to make peace if the Waldenses would comply with certain conditions. But the people would not be deceived again, and the messengers returned to the count to report that the Vaudois were prepared to fight.

The Waldenses now felt ready for the attack which they expected at any time. They stationed scouts on the mountain tops to watch the movements of enemy soldiers. They organized "flying squadrons," groups of men ready to rush at a moment's notice to any point under attack. With each of these went two pastors who prayed with the soldiers before battle. These pastors would also care for the wounded, pray for the dying, and urge the Waldenses to be merciful in the day of victory.

Knowing that they could never hope to defend all their valleys, the larger part of the nation once more gathered in the village of Pra del Tor in the valley of Angrogna. With them came their women and children, their cattle, goats and sheep, and as much food as they could carry.

Realizing that if he could conquer this valley the rest of the fight would be easy, La Trinita decided to make his first attack there. For an entire day his army battled near the entrance to that great stronghold, seeking to overwhelm the defenders of the pass. When the sun went down, the count realized that his soldiers had made no progress, although many had been slain. The next morning he withdrew his troops and discussed with his captains what they should do.

Two weeks later he was ready to make another attack. This time his army would enter the valley from three directions. One body of soldiers would march up the gorge of the Angrogna River. The count hoped that all the Waldenses would rush to fight that group. Meanwhile other troops would cross the mountains and enter the valley from the east, while still a third group would come down from the north. If one attack failed, he felt sure one of the others would succeed.

On the morning of the attack, Vaudois scouts first saw the company marching up the narrow gorge and gave the alarm. Six Waldensian youth ran to the point threatened and waited. As soon as La Trinita's soldiers came in sight, the guns of the Vaudois blazed out with such hot fire into the advancing company that the invaders stopped in confusion. Not more than two soldiers could march along that narrow gorge side by side. As La Trinita's soldier's fell before the guns of the six Vaudois youth, a wall of dead soldiers steadily built up. Then panic seized those still in the gorge and they were unable to move forward. Helpless, they stood in the narrow path, listening to the roar of muskets echo from the canyon walls. Unable to stand the strain longer, with cries of terror they discarded their arms and fled back the way they had come.

Suddenly another alarm sounded. One of the scouts saw the company which had marched over the mountain pass to enter Angrogna from the east. A second group of Waldensian soldiers rushed up the slopes of the mountain, attacked the invaders and forced them to flee back down the mountain.

Meanwhile, the third group had climbed up still another mountain pass endeavoring to enter the valley from the north. Again the scouts gave the alarm, but by now the Waldenses had few soldiers available to send against the new threat. Knowing that the invaders must pass through a narrow defile before entering their valley, the Waldenses scattered themselves in ambush around the mouth of the pass. Weary and out of breath from their long climb and steep descent, the invaders emerged from the defile. Before them lay the beautiful valley. Rushing forward they shouted one to the other.

"Haste, haste, Angrogna is ours."

Then, starting up from their ambush on all sides of the startled invaders, the Waldenses fell upon them like a whirlwind. Knowing that the Vaudois had fewer soldiers than they, the Piedmontese fought desperately, and the battle raged furiously. But soon Waldensian soldiers who had been victorious at other points in the valley came hurrying to aid their brethren. They defeated the invaders, killing many and chasing the rest back over the mountains they had so recently crossed.

Count La Trinita, furious that all three of his attacking companies had been defeated, jeered at his men.

"What is the matter with you?" he asked. "Those Waldenses aren't soldiers, they are simple farmers who don't know how to fight!"

"If those men don't know how to fight, then neither do we!" replied the men.

Once again La Trinita withdrew his army to the plains of Piedmont. He decided to wait for reinforcements before trying again. He did not have long to wait. The king of Spain sent a regiment; so did the king of France. Soon he had seven thousand men. Setting his army in motion he once more started for the mountains, determined to wipe out the disgrace of his former defeats.

For the third time he directed his main attack against the valley of Angrogna. One Sunday morning the whole Waldensian community gathered for worship on a wide grassy slope. The valley echoed to songs of the people. The pastors again read to them the promises of God. Once more they pledged never to surrender their faith.

Suddenly a young scout rushed, breathless into the assembly, pointing to the surrounding mountains. Looking up, the people saw La Trinita's soldiers entering the valley from three directions at the same time.

A few Waldensian men hurried to the place where the dark gorge of the Angrogna River opened up into the valley and there halted one group of the invaders and turned them back. Strong barricades erected earlier by the Waldenses

stopped the other two groups. As La Trinita's men struggled to cross over the barricades, the Waldenses fought to
push them back. The battle raged for hours, and by the
end of the day the soldiers realized that their attempt to
enter the valley had failed again.

Some of La Trinita's finest captains died in the battle.
The count himself, present at the fighting, is said to have
sat down and wept when he saw the bodies of his dead
soldiers heaped in piles. Never again did he jeer at his
men for not defeating the simple mountaineers. With his
own eyes he had seen them fight. Quietly during the night
La Trinita withdrew his army and returned to the plains.

Discouraged, the count wished he had never tried to
conquer the heretics. But he determined to make one last
effort to restore his lost reputation. At his suggestion, the
duke of Savoy requested the Waldenses to send deputies
to Turin to discuss peace terms with the prince.

At this same time, La Trinita assembled all his soldiers
and led them by a night march once more against the
Pra del Tor, hoping to surprise the Waldenses. With their
deputies discussing peace terms in Turin, they would not
be likely to suspect an attack. With a word of encourage-
ment to each of his captains, La Trinita sent his army
once more up the narrow, two-mile gorge leading to the
valley he had tried for months to capture.

Morning services had just ended and the Waldenses
were scattering to their various duties when a shout of
warning went up.

"The gorge! The gorge! Soldiers are coming up the gorge!"

With no time to gather the entire Vaudois company together, a handful of brave mountaineers took up muskets and ran to the point of greatest danger. As the first
two of the enemy turned into the valley from the mouth
of the gorge, the Vaudois shot them down. The next two
fell likewise on top of their companions. Then two more

fell. Calmly the Waldenses kept firing and reloading their muskets. The wall of dead rose higher and higher until the soldiers in the pass could not go forward.

As in former years, some of the Vaudois climbed the slopes of the mountain overlooking the gorge. Soon great stones came crashing down on the Piedmontese soldiers, crushing dozens of them where they stood. It is not surprising that once again, terrible panic overwhelmed those who remained. They tried to flee, but the path was too narrow. Scores of soldiers were pushed over the edge of the cliff to their death on the rocks beside the stream.

La Trinita and some of his officers camped two miles away. As his army set out the night before, he had vowed that before the day ended his soldiers would turn the river red with the blood of the Waldenses. About the middle of the morning, one of his men came to him in great excitement.

"The Angrogna is turning red!" he shouted.

"It is the blood of the heretics," explained the jubilant general, "Pra del Tor has fallen and the blood of the heretics flows in the river!"

But before long, a few soldiers who had escaped from the gorge staggered into the Piedmontese camp, bringing word of the destruction of another army. Once more La Trinita learned that his efforts to enter the valley of Angrogna had failed. The blood in the river was that of his own soldiers. That same day he gathered his remaining soldiers together and marched away. He never returned.

The peace talks continued, and in the end the duke of Savoy called off the war. He no longer insisted that these people he had failed to conquer return to the church of Rome. He returned all their lands to them.

Almost a hundred years would pass before another great effort would be made to destroy them. Let us now turn back two hundred years, and see what the Waldenses in another part of Italy had been doing.

8

One Light Went Out

Rain splashed against the windows of the inn. The wind blew in gusts, rattling the shutters. Occasionally an extra strong blast came down the chimney, driving smoke into the room and scattering ashes over the floor. Before the sputtering fire sat two young men from the Waldensian valleys. They had come on business to the city of Turin, the capital of Piedmont. The next day they would return to their homes in the mountains.

"I wish it were possible to find work here in Turin," one remarked wistfully.

"Why, have you lost your love for the mountains?"

"Oh, no, I could never do that. But life there becomes harder every year. My father's farm is small, and I have four brothers. What will we do for land? How can we marry and live in our village when the farms are already too small to support us?"

The other youth nodded solemnly.

"What you say is true. I too have thought of the problem. But you would not dare work here in Turin. The priests would soon discover that you were not attending mass, and you would not live long."

A stranger who had just finished his supper lounged at the table not far from the fire. He had been listening to the conversation between the two young men. Now he stood, walked over and joined them.

"Excuse my interrupting," he said in the melodious tone of an Italian from the southern part of the peninsula.

"If you will trust me, I can take you to a place where good farm land abounds. We do not have enough inhabitants to cultivate it, however, so you would be welcome."

"Where is this wonderful land?" asked one of the young men, astonished.

"It is in the southern part of Italy, and is called Calabria. I live there myself, and I can assure you that the nobles there would welcome honest, industrious citizens like yourselves."

"The only problem would concern our religion," remarked one of the young men gravely. "You see, we do not belong to the Church of Rome."

The stranger smiled. "Heretics, are you? Well, I can't say I am too faithful a Catholic myself. However, I think this problem could be worked out. The king of Naples rules very tolerantly over Calabria. Provided you pay your taxes faithfully, you would have nothing to fear. You could even elect your own magistrates. What do you think about it?"

"We are not in a position to give you an answer immediately. We must return home, lay this plan before our pastors and elders and see what they think about it. Will you be visiting Turin for a while so we can return and discuss this suggestion further?"

"I expect to be here for about three months yet, and the landlord of this inn can always tell you where to find me.

Handing one of the young men a piece of paper on which he had written his name, the stranger bowed and returned to his own table.

A few days later, the young men returned to their valley home in the Alps. They talked enthusiastically with the older men about the stranger's suggestion. Fifty years earlier such an idea would have been instantly rejected, but conditions had greatly changed during the past decade. The terrible persecution of the Albigenses in France had resulted in thousands of refugees crossing the Alps and settling among the Waldenses. Although they carefully cultivated every bit of good land in the valleys, yet hunger sometimes entered their homes, particularly during the long, cold winters. More than once the families had to fall back on the chestnuts which grew plentifully along the streams for their winter diet.

"Why not send two of our best men to spy out the land as the Israelites did before entering Canaan?" one of the pastors suggested. "They can return and tell us whether the land is fertile; they can also discover the best way of getting there. If the land proves fertile and the government tolerant this could be a great blessing to us. Besides, in that far land there may be people to whom we can carry the gospel."

The people therefore chose two good citizens who traveled down through Italy to Calabria, to look over the country. They returned with glowing reports.

"All kinds of fruit trees clothe the beautiful hills," they said. "On the plains grow vineyards and chestnuts. On the rising ground we found walnuts and many types of useful trees. Grass grows thick and our animals would flourish. We talked with some of the people living there now, and they told us they rarely see snow in winter. Altogether it is a very rich country with only a few inhabitants."

Before long a large group of emigrants set out from the valleys which for generations had been their home. They carried with them a Bible translation in their own language. It took several weeks to make the long journey. Their household furniture was piled high on crude carts, pulled by beasts of burden. Their cattle, sheep and goats followed at the rear of the procession.

Upon arriving in the new country, two of the leaders went to Naples to talk with King Ferdinand, who drew up a treaty granting the strangers a certain portion of his territory. Here they might live freely, rule themselves, and worship as they pleased.

Soon the area began to change. It became one of the most fruitful and prosperous sections of the king's dominions.

The king and the marquis of Spinello were overjoyed as they watched the country prosper, and noted how wealthy the Waldenses became. The prompt manner in which the Waldenses paid all taxes particularly pleased them.

In order to avoid trouble with the all-powerful Church of Rome, the Waldenses even consented to pay tithes which the priests demanded. During the following half century, several companies followed the first pioneer settlers into the warm and fertile southland.

In order that the religious faith of the Waldenses in Calabria should not grow dim, pastors came regularly from the Alps to minister in the churches, each remaining for two or three years. Then they returned and new ones came. The pope in Rome knew about these heretical settlements, but the people lived peacefully and quietly and paid their tithes faithfully. The king of Naples and the local nobles found it profitable to allow the Waldensian settlers to live in their country. More peaceful decades passed.

Then came the time of the Protestant Reformation. Germany, parts of Switzerland, all of Denmark, Norway, and Sweden broke away from the Roman Church and refused to pay her any more money or to obey the commands of the pope. When the news reached the settlements in Calabria, the people rejoiced. They could hardly believe that people now could freely preach the true gospel of Jesus in many parts of Europe.

The missionary spirit began to stir anew the hearts of the Waldenses in Calabria. They became convinced that they had a duty to teach the people living in neighboring towns and villages about the love of Jesus, and that praying to the saints and confessing their sins to a priest was not necessary. They also began to question their practice of paying tithes to the papal church. They wrote to the home church in the Alps asking that some missionary pastors be sent to them.

The pastors in the valleys wondered who to send. Then they remembered an Italian who had passed through their valleys two years before on his way to study in Calvin's school in Geneva. They sent a message, inviting him to go as a missionary pastor to the settlements in Calabria. The young man, Jean Paschale, was not blind to the dangers he would meet. He well knew that any effort to spread Protestant teachings in Italy would bring down the anger of the state church.

"Why should you be the one chosen to go?" asked his beautiful fiancée, Camilla Geurina.

"It is my own country," replied Paschale sorrowfully; "I know the language, and those people are my people."

Paschale decided to accept the appointment and prepared to leave. When the sad day of his departure came, Camilla walked with him along the road. Finally they had to separate. Throwing her arms around his neck, she exclaimed sorrowfully "Alas, so near to Rome, and so far from me."

Standing there she watched her beloved until he passed a bend in the road. Sorrowfully she returned home, never to see him again.

When Jean arrived in Calabria, he immediately began preaching. Boldly be entered nearby towns and villages, and with Bible in hand taught the people, warning them against the false teachings of the Church of Rome. The priests became enraged. A group of them went to the marquis of Spinello, demanding that the heretics be punished. Very reluctantly the marquis commanded all the Waldenses in his area, with their pastors, to appear before him.

When Paschale with his flock gathered before the nobleman, the marquis spoke sharply to them, arrested the pastor, and dismissed his followers, demanding that they must conform to the teachings of the Roman Church. He had Paschale taken to Naples and bound with cruel cords so tight they cut into the flesh of his arms and legs. Then his captors threw him into a dark and filthy dungeon.

While he was in the dungeon, one of his brothers, a Catholic, came to visit him. Their meeting was sad indeed. Bartholomeo appealed to Jean to recant his errors and enter the Church of Rome. He offered half his fortune if Jean would only renounce his faith; but he pleaded in vain. Paschale was prepared to die for his faith, but he would never give it up.

From that dungeon Paschale wrote to his fiancee, pointing out that they would probably not meet again on earth, but urging her to be faithful to the gospel and reminding her that they would meet in heaven. Shortly after this Paschale was taken to Rome where he was thrown into a dungeon even worse than the one he had occupied in Naples.

Having removed the pastor, the marquis and the inquisitor who had been sent down from Rome to stamp out heresy, thought there would be little trouble with the Waldenses. First the inquisitor called the people of San Sexto together and told them they must either attend mass or be destroyed. He gave them until the next morning to decide.

Silently, during the dark hours of the night, the company slipped away to take refuge in the forest. The inquisitor went on to the next city. There he had the city gates closed so no one could take to the forests. Then he called the people together and told them that the people of San Sexto had all agreed to attend mass. He commanded them to likewise submit to the church.

Believing what they heard, the people consented to listen to mass. Then the gates of the town were thrown open and they learned that they had been deceived. Mourning over their weakness, they determined to join their friends from San Sexto in the woods, but their marquis, with promises of reform, finally persuaded them to stay.

The inquisitor sent two companies of armed men against the people of San Sexto. The soldiers tracked some of the people to their eaves and killed them. But the many rocks rolled down on the soldiers by the Waldenses discouraged them from climbing very far after the heretics. The inquisitor next called for more soldiers, and a larger company gathered around the Waldenses now firmly entrenched in a fort.

As the Waldenses had little food left, they decided to try to make peace with their enemies. Under a flag of truce, one of their leaders went into the camp of the papal army.

"If you will let us go peacefully," he told the soldiers, "we will pass through Italy to our old homes in the north, never to trouble you again." But the soldiers showed no interest.

"That you may not do," they told him. "You must either surrender and give up your faith, or be destroyed."

The messenger returned with the sad tidings. "We can do nothing but defend ourselves until we die. We cannot and will not give up our faith."

Again the soldiers advanced, only to be met by a heavier shower of stones and rocks than before. The rocks killed some soldiers and injured many more.

Then the army viceroy issued an edict, promising to pardon all bandits, outlaws, and criminals willing to join in another effort to reduce the Waldenses in their stronghold. In response to his invitation, a large number of men gathered. They knew of secret paths through the mountains, and they used this knowledge to approach the fort from every side. Clambering over great rocks, they rushed the barricades and overwhelmed the brave defenders who were all killed in the struggle. Men, women, and children died together. The soldiers then took over the former homes of the Waldenses and all their possessions. Waldenses from other towns of Calabria were gathered in prisons and killed.

With the destruction of the Vaudois went the prosperity of Calabria. The brigands and robbers knew how to fight and kill, but they did not know how to farm the land or take care of the animals. Gradually the settlements of the Waldenses in Calabria disappeared.

The last act of the tragedy took place in Rome.

One bright spring morning, all the bells in the imperial city began to ring at once. The great drawbridge leading into the courtyard of the castle of Saint Angelo was lowered and the citizens of the city flocked across it by thousands. Soon the people packed the courtyard. On one side sat Pope Pius IV, surrounded by a glittering array of cardinals, bishops, and priests. In the center of the yard a scaffold stood with an iron stake, a chain, and a bundle of firewood on it.

After the courtyard had filled, an iron door leading from an underground dungeon slowly opened. The spectators heard the clank of chains, as a young man, his pale and haggard face showing the marks of suffering, shuffled across the yard and toward the scaffold.

"Heretic! Heretic! Child of the devil!" The shouts came from all sides. A storm of hissing greeted the young prisoner as he dragged his chains across to the scaffold, then staggered slowly up the steps. When he reached the platform, he turned and faced the people. As he lifted his chain-covered hands, a great silence fell over the crowd.

"Good people," said Jean Paschale, the prisoner, I am come here today to die for confessing my belief in my divine Master and Saviour, Jesus Christ.

Gladly do I give my life for Him who gave His life for me."

He then turned and directly faced the pope. Gesturing toward the pontiff, he accused him of being the murderer of the children of God, the enemy of the gospel of Christ, and summoned him and all his cardinals one day to appear before the judgment bar of God where they would be sentenced for their crimes against those who loved Jesus.

The pope and his cardinals, made uncomfortable by his attack, motioned for the executioner to hasten the death. The executioner fastened Paschale to the stake, set a torch to the wood, and watched the flames consume him. His ashes were gathered up and cast into the river Tiber which carried them to the Mediterranean Sea.

9

Storms and Plagues

While Paschale and his followers suffered in Calabria, the Waldenses in the Alpine valleys had been struggling against Count La Trinita and his army. Not until June 5, 1561, nine months after Paschale's execution in Rome, did the duke of Savoy sign a peace treaty with the Vaudois. Now the people who had sheltered in Pra del Tor for so many months left in small groups for their home valleys.

Most families experienced sad homecomings. The Piedmontese soldiers had burned their houses, torn up their farms, and wrecked their orchards. They had cut down vineyards and filled wells with dirt. But the loss in battle of many of their sturdiest young men caused the Waldenses their greatest sorrow. Many years passed before the scars of that war disappeared and prosperity returned to the valleys.

A lack of food became the people's most urgent problem. The time for planting crops had passed by the time the fighting ended in mid-summer. When autumn arrived, they had pitifully little to reap. At this time, too, a few penniless stragglers arrived from the desolated colonies in Calabria and sorrowfully told of the extermination of their people. The Vaudois made them welcome, but it meant more mouths to feed during that first long hard winter following the war.

The Protestant nations had watched the Waldenses' struggle with interest and anxiety. When news of their empty granaries reached the leaders of Protestant countries, they lost no time in sending help. The great reformer John Calvin, still living in Geneva, took the lead in collecting food and clothing for the needy Protestants. Many of the German princes likewise made collections. Without this timely aid, the Waldenses would have died from starvation during that winter.

But still more troubles came to the Waldenses. The duke of Savoy felt deeply humiliated because his armies had failed to conquer the farmers in the mountains. The duke sent Castrocaro, who had been a colonel under La Trinita, as governor of the valleys. He had been captured once by Waldensian forces, treated kindly and then released. But in his heart burned a feeling of rage, even against those who had been merciful to him.

Before Castrocaro assumed his new duties, he received instructions from two individuals. First the kind-hearted duchess, herself a Protestant, begged him to protect her people in the mountains. His second visitor, the archbishop of Turin, urged him to do everything in his power to convert the heretics to Catholicism. The governor gave his word that he would do his best.

As soon as the new governor arrived at La Torre, which he chose as his capital, he began to make trouble for his subjects. First he commanded them to send away many of their finest pastors. Next he sent a false report to the duke that the Waldenses were preparing to rebel and renew the war. The duke promptly sent the governor an extra regiment of soldiers to enable him to preserve peace in the mountains. The governor then built strong forts to guard the entrances of the valleys.

To the weary Waldenses these restrictions sometimes seemed harder to bear than open warfare. They sent messengers to the duke in Turin, pointing out their mistreatment, and begging for an end to their troubles. But the governor had so poisoned the mind of the duke that he spoke roughly to them, accused them of preparing to break the peace, and sent them back with no hope of change. This made the governor bolder than ever. He sent out notices that soon the Waldenses would have to decide whether they would return to the ancient church, or accept death.

In their troubles the people again thought of their powerful friends in Germany. They sent appeals, begging the princes to intervene and try to persuade the duke to treat them justly. The sad story stirred the heart of Frederick, elector of the Palatinate, to pity for his brethren in the mountains. He wrote a strong letter reminding the duke that God hears the cries of the oppressed. "Let your highness take care not voluntarily to make war upon God," he wrote, "and not to persecute Christ in His members. Let your highness consider that the Christian religion was established by persuasion, and not by violence."

We do not know whether the duke answered the elector's letter. But be did change his methods. The governor stopped his threats and harassments. When the duke died, his son took his place. His mother urged him to investigate what the governor had been doing. When this was done and the man's wickedness discovered, the duke sent soldiers to arrest him. Hearing of this, Castrocaro gathered a band of desperate men around him and fled for refuge to a strong castle. For a time he defended himself well, but finally had to surrender. Soldiers escorted him to Turin where he was sentenced to prison, there to spend the last years of his life.

For the next fifty years, the Waldenses lived without war. The year 1629, however, brought calamities which nearly destroyed them. First, a cloudburst among some of the higher mountains caused flooded rivers which swept away homes, cattle, sheep, and people. In September an icy wind blew down the valleys, uprooting the groves of chestnut trees, whose fruit had served the Waldenses well in times of famine. A second cloudburst which completely ruined the grape crop followed almost immediately.

The Vaudois pastors met together for a session of fasting and prayer. As they discussed their problems they little realized that a storm far worse than any previous calamities would soon break over their valleys.

A French army under Marshal Schonberg marched into the valleys that summer, occupying them for several weeks. Unfortunately many of Schonberg's soldiers had come from areas in France infested with plague. Soon this dreadful disease attacked the mountain people. During the hot months of July and August they fell like grain from the sickle. Four of the pastors died in July, and seven in August. This left only three pastors; one in Lucerna, one in San Martin, and one at Perosa. These three pastors met in the valley of Angrogna to discuss how to provide further spiritual leadership for their stricken people. They decided to ask the Swiss Protestant church in Geneva to send them men of God who could replace their fallen pastors.

That winter the plague lessened, but the following spring it raged more violently than ever. One of the three surviving pastors died. Entire families lay down and died together. Reports estimate that from one half to two thirds of the total valley population fell before that plague. Not enough workers survived to harvest the wheat crop. Grapes rotted on the vines. Towns and villages which had been scenes of busy industry now lay silent. One pastor lost four of his sons. Passing in and out of the homes of the sick and dying, this man of God, Pierre Gilles, lived through the plague to care for his afflicted people.

The Protestant church in Switzerland responded to the appeal from the Vaudois and sent a number of pastors. They determined that the gospel light in the valleys should not be allowed to flicker and die. The new pastors spoke only the French language and conducted all their services in that tongue. The Vaudois soon learned to understand because their own tongue was a mixture of French and Italian. They no longer called their pastors barbe, but ministers. They loved the Swiss ministers for their gentle ways and kindly deeds.

The century of peace drew to a close. Could the Waldenses look into the future, they would behold still blacker clouds gathering. On the throne of Savoy sat Charles Emmanuel II, an inexperienced youth. The throne of France held Louis XIV, the most powerful king of the century. Between them, these two rulers would bring the Waldenses to the brink of destruction.

One of the soldiers seized Marie in his arms, mounted his horse, and galloped away before anyone could stop them.

10

Gold Coins for the Marquis

Not all Waldenses lived in mountain valleys. Some of them lived in villages in the foothills of the Alps and along the banks of streams which flowed from the valleys. Catholics also lived in these villages. In one of them lived a little Waldensian girl named Marie. She had a Catholic playmate, whose home she often visited and whose parents treated her kindly. Marie's parents did not mind her visiting a Catholic home because they felt that she understood her Bible too well for her religious beliefs to be shaken.

One day the mother of the Catholic child took little Marie into their village's large Catholic church and showed her beautiful pictures, images, candles, and an altar laden with golden cloths. Marie had never seen anything like that, and thought it all looked very beautiful. Frequently after that, the Catholic mother asked Marie whether she would like to become a Catholic. But the little Waldensian girl only shook her head. The mother decided to change her methods.

"Unless you promise to become a Catholic someday, I cannot allow you to come and play with my little girl," she told Marie one morning. "The priest will be very angry if he finds out that my daughter is playing with a heretic. Come, just promise me that some day you will become a Catholic."

Marie became frightened, but she did wish to continue to play with her friend. So she replied, "My mother and my father would not like it if I said that."

"They will never hear of it from me, and you must not say a word about it, either. Come, just say that someday you will become a Catholic."

Marie looked at the woman's smiling face. Then she slowly nodded her head.

"Very well. When you are older, I will have the priest come and teach you all the things you will need to know. Now run and play."

Marie tried not to show the worry that troubled her when she returned home. Not for the world would she want her parents to know of the promise she had made their Catholic neighbor. Her daily visits continued, but somehow much of the joy had gone out of them. Then one day to her terror, she found the priest there, waiting to baptize her with some holy water he had brought.

"No, no, not yet! I couldn't be baptized today. Just wait a little longer!"

"Do you know what will happen if you die before I baptize you into the true church?" asked the priest.

Trembling, Marie could only shake her head.

"You will go straight to hell and burn there forever and never get out. Think it over. When I come back next time, you must be ready for baptism."

Marie felt really frightened this time. Her mother soon saw that something had upset her daughter. For a while Marie refused to answer her mother's many questions. After a while, she burst into tears and told all about her talks with the Catholic woman and the priest. Greatly alarmed, the mother told her husband all that had happened. Both knew that for many years the Piedmontese had kidnaped Vaudois children and carried them off to monasteries and nunneries in the plain to be brought up as Catholics.

Fearful lest his daughter be taken away, Marie's father first forbade her visiting her friend's house any more. At the same time he arranged for her to be taken by night to stay with a relative in a distant village where she remained for several months.

In the autumn, after the grapes had been gathered, the people of the village where Marie had gone celebrated a festival. Marie's parents came for the occasion and to visit with their little girl. How glad they were to see their child well and happy. They had a good time that day until suddenly they saw a band of about thirty armed men on horses galloping swiftly toward them. When the soldiers reached the circle of villagers they dismounted. One of them rushed forward, seized Marie in his arms, and rushed away before the terrified people could do anything to stop them. Then the soldiers galloped down the valley and disappeared in the dusky night.

During the weeks and months which followed, the sad parents tried in every possible way to discover where Marie had been taken. None of the magistrates would talk of the matter with the father and mother. As the months dragged into years, the parents gave up hope of ever again seeing or hearing from their daughter.

Seven years later the father heard that Marie, now a young lady, lived in a convent at Novara, where she had become a Catholic nun. Only after she had taken all her vows did the nuns allow Marie to write her mother a letter. The sad parents, reading the letter, realized that someone had told her what to write. They knew that they would never learn the whole story. Still they felt relieved to know that their daughter was alive.

Marie's mother realized, however, that she would never see her child again. As a result of her continual grieving her health failed and she developed tuberculosis. Then when Marie would have been twenty years old, the abbess wrote that the girl had died of a fever. Her broken-hearted mother died soon after. Years later it was learned that her kidnappers had given her a choice when she reached the age of eighteen. She could either marry a young Catholic nobleman with a large fortune, or become a nun. Since she refused to marry, she was forced to become a nun.

What happened to Marie happened also to hundreds of other Vaudois children. Their parents, crushed with grief, often traced their children to Catholic homes in Turin and other nearby towns. When they begged to have their children back, they always received the same answer.

"If you will become Catholics and be baptized into the true church, we will return your children."

Sadly the bereaved parents would make their way back to their lonely homes without their boys and girls. No record exists of any Waldensian giving up his faith in order to regain a son or daughter.

In 1622, Pope Gregory XV established a new society in the Catholic Church, the Society for the Propagation of the Faith. Its purpose was to wipe out heretics, either by bringing them into the Catholic Church or by exterminating them. Within a few years the society had spread through Spain, France, and Italy.

In every Catholic city and town in Europe people collected money for this society. Priests used the money to bribe people who happened to be in trouble. When they heard of a Protestant businessman going bankrupt, they would offer him a large sum if he would be baptized into the Roman Church. If an unlucky Protestant traveler was arrested and thrown into a dungeon, the priests would visit him, offering him freedom, plus a sum of money if he would be baptized into the Catholic Church.

By 1650 a branch of this society had been established in Turin, the capital of the kingdom of Savoy. Its members determined that the Waldenses who lived close by would either accept the Catholic faith or be destroyed.

The marchioness de Pianeza became one of the chief supporters of this society in Turin. In her youth she had not been well-behaved, and her conscience troubled her. The priest told her that if she would devote her time and wealth to the great task of converting heretics, all her sins would be forgiven. So she gave much of her money to the Society for the Propagation of the Faith and the Extermination of Heretics.

To start the work of winning back the Waldenses, the marchioness sent a group of Capuchin monks to preach to the heretics in the valleys. At first these men thought they would easily convert the Vaudois, and boldly challenged the pastors to public discussions. But the ministers knew their Bibles, and could easily prove the monks wrong. Embarrassed, the monks returned to Turin and sadly reported to the marchioness de Pianeza that they had made no converts. They blamed their failure on the Vaudois pastors.

The marchioness called the members of her council together to see what new plan they might make to eradicate heresy in Savoy.

"Can we persuade the duke that it is his sacred duty to destroy this nest of heretics?" asked one angry priest.

"No," replied the lady. I know he has decided not to break the peace of his kingdom by attacking the Waldenses."

"If only the heretics would do something rash that might arouse the anger of the duke!"

I fear you will wait a long time for that. They live very peaceably."

After discussing the situation for a long time, one of the monks finally thought of a plan which they decided might work. The next day this monk found two men who agreed to go into the valleys and try to goad the Waldenses into some rash move.

These men disguised themselves and pretended to be Vaudois travelers. Once in the mountain valley, they attended a meeting of one of the general councils. They told the people that the duke planned to raise an army with which to destroy them. The convent of Capuchin monks, they said, was a nest of spies, plotting their destruction. Then another man, whom these strangers had bribed, joined in, saying that he had also heard of this and knew it to be true.

"Let us storm the monastery, expel the monks and burn the building," urged one of the spies. "Thus we can show the duke that we do not sleep and cannot be slaughtered like sheep."

A few hotheads among the company agreed. That very night they appeared before the monastery, expelled the monks and set fire to the building. News of this action quickly reached the duke. Naturally, he grew angry when he learned of it, but the marchioness and her council were delighted. At last there would be war. The duke summoned an army of six thousand men to march to Villaro and wipe out all its Protestant inhabitants.

News of this reached Leger, the wisest and best of the Waldensian pastors. He immediately went to Villaro where he collected positive proof that the men who had plotted the deed were in the pay of the Society of the Propagation of the Faith. With this evidence he went to Turin and laid it before the surprised duke, who immediately canceled his plans for punishing the Waldenses. Members of the society, deeply angered that their plan had failed, determined to make yet another attempt to provoke the Waldenses to violence.

The Protestants at Villaro worked hard and soon repaired the monastery which had been damaged by fire. The monks returned and vowed to destroy the Protestant church there. Since that church lay not far from their monastery, they started digging a tunnel which would lead them directly under the Protestant sanctuary. They planned to drag several barrels of gunpowder directly under the Waldensian meetinghouse. Then when the congregation filled the building, they would set fire to the explosives, blow up the building and everybody in it.

This dreadful plan might have succeeded had not a woman walking along the village street one morning heard a pounding noise coming directly from under her feet. She went to the mayor of the town, relating what she had heard. Though disbelieving her story, he agreed to investigate. With the woman as a guide, the two returned the next morning to the spot. They set a drum on the ground directly over the noise which they could hear distinctly. Placing a coin on the drumhead, they saw to their surprise that it moved regularly. Muffled thuds could be heard through the earth beneath them.

An investigation of nearby buildings soon revealed the tunnel, and they thus averted a dreadful disaster. Yet this event filled the Waldensians with fear as they realized that their enemies would stop at nothing in their efforts to destroy them.

Next the marchioness went to Duke Charles Emmanuel II, demanding that he issue an edict banishing many of the most important Waldensian pastors from the country. Since the duke had just received some threatening letters from the pope, he agreed and issued the decree. This forced some of the pastors to flee to Switzerland, some to Holland, and others to Germany.

About this time some new laws were passed to trouble the Vaudois. The laws closed their churches and ordered the Protestant towns of Bobbio, Villaro, Angrogna, and Rora to build mission houses for the Capuchin monks and supply them with food. They forbade any foreigner to come to the valleys under pain of death. This law was designed to prevent new pastors from Switzerland replacing those who had died of the plague or been banished.

Not long after this the marchioness de Pianeza became very sick, and she realized she would soon die. On her deathbed, she sent for her husband from whom she had been separated for many years. Wondering what she might want with him, the marquis entered the sick room. She greeted him and then explained her trouble.

"I greatly fear that I shall be punished because I have not been able to convert the heretics in the valleys. I cannot die in peace unless you promise that you will carry on the work of the society, and never give up until the Waldensian heretics have returned to the true church. Will you accept this responsibility?"

The marquis hesitated. This was not exactly a task he would have chosen.

"I have deposited a large sum of money with the archbishop," continued the marchioness, "and have instructed him to give it to you when the valleys are cleared of heretics. Please promise that you will do this for me."

The eyes of the marquis opened wide in surprise. He considered this to be good news, indeed. He reached out his hand and took that of the dying woman.

"It shall be as you wish. I shall faithfully fulfill your desires."

A few hours later the marchioness died. The marquis determined to win the fortune awaiting him in the palace of the archbishop with as little delay as possible. And he knew of only one quick method to convert the heretics; that was to kill them.

Hastening to the duke, he persuaded him to issue an edict commanding all Vaudois living in Lucerna, Fenile, Bubiana, Bricherasio, San Giovannie, and La Torre to quit their ancient homes and retire into the central valleys of Bobbio, Angrogna, and Rora within twenty days or be put to death. That edict deprived the Waldenses of their most fertile lands. The edict went on to say that those who would renounce their Protestant faith need not move.

This decree, issued on January 25, 1655, in the middle of winter, caused the Vaudois great hardship. Snow lay deep in the valleys, floods swelled the rivers, and ice covered the mountains. But not one family among the thousands living in the districts included in the edict agreed to remain in their homes and attend mass. Instead, families took apart their heavy articles of furniture, tied their scanty supplies of food and clothing in bundles, and with flocks of sheep and goats, trudged out of the towns where their ancestors had lived for centuries. They fled to the Vaudois who were living in more favored areas.

The Vaudois discussed their plight. They did not have enough land in their three remaining valleys to raise food for the entire nation. Surely, they thought, their prince could not realize how impossible it would be for them to live there, crowded together.

Again they chose a group of the wisest men of the nation and sent them to Turin to plead with the duke. Some of his officers listened to their sad story. Long years before, the Vaudois leaders pointed out, their fathers had signed treaties with former dukes giving them the right to live in the other towns and valleys. Did the duke now intend to violate those treaties? They described the pitiful condition of the fugitives and pointed out the tragedy which faced the nation if the duke did not allow it more land on which to live.

Alas, the ear of the prince had been poisoned with lies. He would not even meet them. But his officers assured the Vaudois that the matter would be considered. With this promise they had to be satisfied.

Then the Waldenses were detained in Turin until April 17, as their enemies did not wish them to return and alarm the people of the valleys whom they hoped to take by surprise. That very night at midnight, the marquis de Pianeza secretly slipped out of Turin at the head of an army of fifteen thousand men. He wanted more than ever to win the gold crowns his wife had left with the archbishop.

11

Eighteen Men
Against a Thousand

La Torre, the largest of the Waldensian towns, lay at the junction of three rivers. One flowed down from the valley of Angrogna, and one from the valley of Rora. The main stream, the Pelice, arrived after watering the valley of Lucerna. The appearance of the marquis de Pianeza and his army near this town made the inhabitants uneasy.

The marquis' army consisted principally of Piedmontese soldiers with some regiments lent by the French government. He also had two thousand Irish exiles whom Cromwell had expelled from their country, The Waldenses had only three thousand arms-bearing men to face the marquis' fifteen thousand soldiers.

The marquis de Pianeza discovered that the men of La Torre had erected a barricade guarding the principal entrance to the town. He ordered his men to storm it immediately, but so strongly did the Vaudois defend it that after several hours of severe fighting, he called off the attack. During the night a group of Piedmontese slipped around to the other side of the town. In the morning they attacked the Waldenses on two sides. The outnumbered Waldenses escaped along an unguarded road into the mountains with the loss of only a few soldiers.

News of the fighting traveled swiftly to even the most remote Vaudois villages. Men left their farms, seized muskets, swords, or sling shots if they had no better weapons, and hastened to the points threatened, ready to face the foe and protect their families.

The marquis sent out numerous armed patrols in various directions, attempting to capture the valleys. Some of these regiments succeeded in surprising the villagers. They burned their homes, killed men and women, and carried their children away to Catholic schools in Turin and other towns on the plain. More often, however, the Waldenses succeeded in defeating their enemies, although outnumbered sometimes as much as ten to one. Companies of Piedmontese soldiers returned to La Torre reporting losses of five and six hundred men. The soldiers failed to force an entrance into any of the major valleys.

De Pianeza began to wonder whether he would ever win the fortune his wife had left him. He had read of the doomed expeditions of Cataneo and La Trinita in former times. Perhaps his mission might end in failure, too.

Like La Trinita before him, he decided to resort to trickery. On Wednesday morning, April 21, with a blare of trumpets, heralds from the marquis appeared before the surprised Waldensian entrenchments. On being asked what they wanted, they stated that the Vaudois should send deputies to headquarters to talk with the marquis who did not wish to shed blood, but only to restore peace. The marquis, they said, was prepared to make a settlement which would be satisfactory to everyone. This sounded like good news to the farmer-soldiers, so the next day their deputies arrived at La Torre to see De Pianeza.

He received the Vaudois with the greatest courtesy and expressed his regrets for the war and the suffering it had caused. The duke of Savoy, he assured them, had given him authority to make peace so that the people might return to their homes without fear or further loss.

"What must we do to establish this peace?" asked the deputies.

"There is only one condition. The duke asks you to receive one regiment of his army into each of your principal valleys to remain there for a time and help maintain order."

The deputies bowed and retired to carry the terms back to the valleys. They called a council, attended by a large number of people. The pastors felt it unwise to allow soldiers to enter the valleys, and urged that this part of the settlement be rejected. But the people, tired of hardship and suffering, wanted peace. The majority easily outvoted the few pastors and sent word to the marquis that they had accepted his terms.

Piedmontese soldiers promptly entered the valleys of Lucerna and Angrogna and stationed themselves in the homes of the Waldenses. The Waldenses had little food now because they still felt the effects of feeding fugitives from the other valleys during the winter. However, they shared what they did have with the soldiers, turned their beds over to them, and acted as courteously as the soldiers would allow. Little did these simple people guess that the soldiers they housed would soon be their murderers.

Three days went by peacefully. De Pianeza posted soldiers at the entrance and exit of each valley to cut off any possible escape. Then at 4 a.m., Saturday, April 24, 1655, guns boomed out from the castle of La Torre. At this signal, the soldiers rose up and began a massacre more cruel than anything ever before recorded of civilized people. No one will ever know how many died in that first awful hour, but cries from tortured people told of hundreds of victims. Smoke from burning homes soon filled the skies. The rushing streams turned pink with blood. As Waldenses tried to flee to the hills, soldiers tracked them down and slaughtered them. These soldiers invented unheard of methods of torture and death for the Waldensian people. Only a few managed to escape over the mountains.

With the massacre ended, De Pianeza next planned to

destroy Rora, a tiny settlement separated from La Torre
by a chain of lofty mountains. News of the massacre could
not reach Rora quickly because of snow-blocked mountain passes. Its people knew only that a peace treaty had
been signed. De Pianeza selected five hundred of his best
soldiers and dispatched them against Rora. He ordered
them to destroy the village and all its people, then to bring
their animals and possessions back to La Torre.

But De Pianeza did not know that in Rora lived Joshua Giavanello, a man of great courage and one of the most remark-
able captains ever to live in the valleys. Glancing up from his
work one morning, Giavanello saw a line of black dots moving
along the path which led into the valley. The captain instantly
realized that these were soldiers and suspected their errand.
Leaving his plow, he picked up his musket and hurried away
to meet the enemy. On his way he picked up six other peas-
ants who agreed to assist him. The little band of seven men
pushed forward along the forest path to meet the five hundred!

Giavanello posted his men where they could ambush
the enemy as they walked through a narrow mountain
pass. Gigantic rocks rose on both sides of the pass.
The Piedmontese soldiers moved carelessly along, never
dreaming of danger from the inhabitants of Rora, a village
of not more than thirty families.

A sudden roar of musket fire startled the soldiers. They
realized they had been discovered. Seven men fell in that
first volley. The others stopped, looked around, but saw
nobody. The muskets spoke again, and more soldiers fell.
Panic seized them, for they had no idea how many attack-
ers there might be.

"Save yourselves! All is lost!" the men shouted as they
turned and fled up the path they had descended. Giavanello followed them for half a mile until he felt sure they
wouldn't return for a while.

That same afternoon some of the older men from Rora

went over the mountain to La Torre and complained to the marquis about the morning attack on their village. De Pianeza pretended to be greatly surprised.

"You did perfectly right to fight off those who attacked you. They must have been bandits, for they were certainly not my soldiers. Go back to your families and fear nothing. I pledge you my honor that no evil shall happen to you."

Giavanello heard these promises, but they did not deceive him. He felt certain that the marquis had ordered the attack, and that he would certainly try again. He therefore enlisted eighteen men who promised to fight with him. Twelve had muskets and swords; the other six had only slings. After posting scouts, the gallant captain waited for the attack.

Sure enough! The next morning one of the scouts spied another group of soldiers entering the valley from a different direction. Again Giavanello placed his men in ambush and waited for the enemy, who marched casually through the forest, not expecting danger. Suddenly they were assailed by a shower of stones from the slings of the Vaudois. The soldiers marched so closely together that not a stone missed its mark. The Piedmontese were preparing to charge when the roar of muskets told them that their enemies had guns as well. The shower of stones became heavier, then the guns spoke again. As on the previous day, the soldiers panicked. Throwing down their arms, they fled up the mountains. The Waldenses pursued them as far as the top of the pass where they dislodged large stones which they sent crashing down the mountainside, inflicting still more losses on the invaders and increasing their terror.

For the second time deputies from Rora went to interview the marquis De Pianeza. This time he did not try to pretend that the soldiers were not his, but rather explained that some charges had been made against the people of Rora, and he had sent his soldiers to investigate. But now he had discovered that the charges were false and they would not be troubled again. They should return to their village and not worry about an attack.

The marquis had become more furious than ever now. He knew that only a handful of men defended Rora, and he determined to capture and destroy it. The next morning a thousand men marched out of La Torre. The company was divided and prepared to enter the valley from different sides. Their numbers were so great that Giavanello decided it would be foolish to try to stop them. He and all the villagers withdrew to a stronghold on the mountainside where they might watch and wait their opportunity to attack.

The Piedmontese arrived, rejoicing that they had met no enemy on the way. They entered the village, plundered it, and seized everything valuable, but found no people. Before leaving Rora, the soldiers set fire to some of the houses. Then laden with booty, they started the return journey to La Torre.

Giavanello had been waiting for a favorable moment. Now it had come. First, though, he knelt down and thanked God who had twice given his men victory. He asked for courage and strength of heart as he prepared to deliver his people from their enemies again.

Following secret paths through the mountains be knew so well, the commander posted his men at strategic points above and in front of the Piedmontese. When the enemy arrived, the Vaudois attacked vigorously. The soldiers of the marquis, thinking all danger past, were caught off guard. They cast aside the booty they had collected and sought only to escape the bullets, arrows, and stones of the Vaudois. Only a few reached La Torre to inform the marquis that his third effort to destroy the people of Rora had also ended in disaster.

In a towering rage, Pianeza ordered his whole army to

prepare to march on Rora. When Captain Mario, the leader of the Irish regiment boasted that with his soldiers he would quickly conquer the little band of heretics, Pianeza gave him permission to prove it.

Pushing boldly forward with his Irishmen, he met with the same catastrophe as the other bands. The Waldenses made a sudden attack from the heights and rolled great stones down onto the soldiers, many of whom were crushed. The captain himself was pushed over the edge of a cliff and fell many feet into a stream. His soldiers managed to rescue him. They carried him, badly wounded, back to La Torre where he died two days later.

Pianeza grew more furious than ever. He had expected to secure wealth, honor, and glory by destroying the heretics in the valleys; instead these farmer-soldiers had defeated thousands of his best troops. Not one of Giavanello's band had fallen into his hands. No wonder the duke of Savoy later complained that the skin of each Waldensian cost him fifteen of his best soldiers.

For the last time, Pianeza assembled his army on the La Torre square, selected three groups of soldiers, numbering ten thousand men altogether, and sent them by three different routes to conquer tiny Rora.

This time Giavanello could not save his overwhelmed village. The inhabitants the soldiers did not kill on the spot, they carried away to be thrust into prison cells. Giavanello and his soldiers managed to escape over the mountains into another valley. Looking back from the top of the pass, the warriors saw the smoke of the burning village, and in their deep grief wondered whether anything could be done to save their people from total destruction.

The prisoners carried off to La Torre included the wife and three daughters of Giavanello. This news delighted Pianeza. He wrote Giavanello the following letter:

"I exhort you for the last time to renounce your heresy.

This is the only hope of your obtaining the pardon of your prince, and of saving the lives of your wife and daughters now my prisoners, and whom, if you continue obstinate, I will burn alive."

In the same letter he also threatened Giavanello, telling him that if he did not surrender, a price would be put on his head.

Giavanello would not surrender his faith, but replied:

"There are no torments so terrible, no death so barbarous that I would not choose rather than deny my Saviour. Your threats cannot cause me to renounce my faith; they only fortify me in it. Should the marquis De Pianeza cause my wife and daughters to pass through the fire, it can but consume their mortal bodies; their souls I commend to God, trusting that He will have mercy on them and on mine, should it please Him that I fall into the marquis' hands."

Did not that letter represent the most severe defeat Giavanello ever inflicted on the marquis? It is not known whether be burned the wife and daughters of Giavanello, but it is known that they never returned to the brave Vaudois commander. With one son whom he had managed to save, Giavanello crossed the Alps into France where he left him in the care of friends. He then returned to his desolate homeland. Having heard of his exploits and admired his bravery, hundreds of fugitive Waldenses flocked to him. The careful drilling he gave made it possible for them to defeat the enemy repeatedly.

Flying squadrons of Vaudois began to attack and cut down small bands of the marquis' soldiers who had wandered from their camps. Many of the Vaudois were killed too, but the people remained unconquered and their spirit unbroken. There is no record of a single one of the Waldenses ever joining the Catholic Church.

The future, however, looked dark to Giavanello and the

brave men with him. How long would it be possible for the fugitives to remain in hiding? Where could they find food? Where would they shelter when summer passed and the bitter cold of winter arrived? Only God could bring deliverance. Day and night hearts and voices lifted in prayer to Him who alone had power to save them from destruction.

Sir Samuel Morland, sent from England, passed through the valleys on his way to Turin, and was shocked at what he saw.

12

Men Who Fight Like Lions

As news spread of the terrible destruction the marquis had caused in the Angrogna and Lucerna valleys, hundreds of Waldenses from other Alpine areas fled from their country. Some climbed over high mountain passes, eventually reaching Switzerland where people in the Protestant countries warmly welcomed them. Especially did Geneva, the city of Calvin, open her homes to the poor fugitives. Other Waldenses fled westward over the Alps into the valleys belonging to France.

The duke of Savoy became enraged to think that his subjects were escaping. He sent a messenger to the French court to protest against the shelter France was giving his "rebellious" subjects and to ask that they be sent back immediately to their own country. Mazarin, who headed the French government during Louis XIV's childhood, replied that it would be impossible in the name of humanity to refuse refuge to the poor fleeing people, even though they were Protestants.

Protestant countries to the north, Germany, Holland, and above all England received news of the massacres with amazement and horror. At first many found it impossible to believe that such deeds could be done by a Christian prince to his own subjects, but the stories of the fugitives as well as reports of eye-witnesses could not be denied. Oliver Cromwell, at the head of the English government, proclaimed a national fast and started a collection to aid the Waldenses. He himself made a personal gift of ten thousand dollars.

Cromwell did even more. He dictated a letter to the duke of Savoy, whose country bordered France, to see that the persecution of the Vaudois stop immediately. He also sent Sir Samuel Morland from his own court to tell the duke to his face that Europe stood horrified at the dreadful deeds his soldiers had done.

The storm his actions had created throughout Europe amazed the duke. At first he tried to deny that any massacres had taken place, but the evidence overwhelmed him. The desolate valleys, burned homes, and hundreds of bodies still lying unburied became proof of his cruelty. Morland, who himself passed through the valleys on his way to Turin, was shocked at what he saw. Standing before the guilty duke and his mother, who had helped instigate the massacres, Morland spoke to the prince as no one had ever dared speak before.

"If all the tyrants of all times and ages were alive again," he said, "they would doubtless be ashamed to find that nothing barbarous nor inhuman, in comparison to these deeds, had ever been invented by them. In the meantime, angels are stricken with horror; men are dizzy with amazement; heaven itself appears astonished with the cries of the dying, and the very earth to blush with the blood of so many innocent persons."

The duke promised to put an end to the persecutions, and Morland left Savoy to visit Switzerland and Germany and find envoys who could go back with him and aid in securing a just peace for the Waldenses.

But meanwhile war continued in the valleys. Giavanello and another patriot, Giaheri, collected bands of Waldenses who turned with fury on the Piedmontese soldiers. So many of the Vaudois had been killed that both bands together numbered only five hundred. Against them were more than fifteen thousand soldiers of the duke of Savoy.

Although few in number, the Waldensian soldiers had one great advantage. They knew every path, every trail, and every stronghold in their valleys. They had another advantage. They fought in a righteous cause and could ask God for help and strength in defending their homes and preserving their ancient faith.

Their enemies, on the other hand, had come into the valleys to kill, destroy, and plunder. They watched with amazement a handful of Waldenses often hurling back powerful forces sent against them, and many became convinced that God did aid the heretics. The Waldenses attacked with such daring, determination, and success, that many of the Piedmontese soldiers lost heart.

The armies waged no large battles now, but scores of small fights in various parts of the valleys. Gradually the numbers of the Vaudois bands increased as volunteers came to join them. Huguenots came from France, and other Protestant soldiers from Switzerland, Germany, Holland, and England.

"I had always considered the Vaudois to be men," said Descombies, a Frenchman who came to help them, "but I found them lions."

Nothing could stop or turn back the Waldenses. They gradually drove their enemies out of the valleys. But when the war passed down onto the plains of Piedmont, the Waldenses lost many of the advantages they had in the mountains. Here the valiant Giavanello was severely wounded in battle and forced to leave the army for nearly two months. The command fell upon Giaheri who sought to uphold the cause of the fallen leader.

One day a man came to Giaheri professing to be a Vaudois. He offered to lead the army to a place where with little effort they might obtain control of a strong fortress. Suspecting nothing unusual, Giaheri and his men pushed forward, not knowing that the guide was a paid traitor. He led the Vaudois directly into an ambush where soldiers of the duke, attacking from all sides in large numbers, completely defeated them. Giaheri himself died in this fight, and by his side fell his gallant son. Despite this severe setback the Waldenses rallied, and soon Giavanello took to the field, leading his soldiers once again to victory.

Commissioners from Louis XIV arrived to arrange terms of peace between the duke and his Protestant subjects. There were also representatives from Switzerland, but deputies from England and the German states had not yet arrived. Unfortunately the Swiss allowed a treaty of peace to be drawn up and hastily signed. By this treaty the Waldenses lost their ancient lands along the right bank of the Pelice River.

Harsh as were the terms of peace, the Waldenses felt relieved to sign them. At least they had peace. Captives were released from prison, and some of the stolen children were returned. Since their country had been so devastated, the government agreed to levy no taxes on the people for five years.

The Waldenses accepted these terms, and the duke pardoned his "rebellious" subjects as he called them, and took them back once more under his protection. But the Waldenses had submitted to a treaty that once more placed them completely under the domination of the duke of Savoy, giving him power to make life easy or hard for them. The duke, deciding to make it impossible for the Waldenses ever again to reject his commands, hastened to build a strong fortress at La Torre, the key town to the valleys.

The next twenty years proved difficult for the Waldenses. Realizing that open persecution would bring down on him the wrath of Protestant Europe, the duke began a series of annoyances. Once again Waldensian children began to disappear, kidnaped and carried away to be reared in monasteries and nunneries. Parents who went to Turin to protest were often seized and thrown into prison themselves. Monks moved into the valleys. They built many new churches and chapels. The duke added new taxes, and these became heavier every year.

Then one year the duke suddenly demanded half a million gold crowns. The Waldenses asked what this levy was for. He told them that the war to conquer them had cost that much and they must now pay for it! The Waldenses protested that they had not rebelled, but had simply fought to protect themselves, their wives, and their children. In their great perplexity they appealed to the king of France! Although Louis XIV became one of the greatest persecutors of Protestants ever to rule in Europe, he was not now prepared to rule against the Waldenses. As a result, the total assessment was cut to 50,000 crowns.

But once again the Waldenses lost many of their best pastors. All during the years of so-called "peace," first one and then another of their leaders was commanded to leave the country and not return. The duke of Savoy and his Catholic advisors realized that the pastors were the leaders of the people. Could they be sent away, then perhaps the will of the people to resist would be weakened.

The Waldenses lost a good friend and defender when Oliver Cromwell died. This Englishman had raised in their behalf more than two hundred thousand dollars. Only half of this amount had been sent to the Waldenses by the time of his death. It had been of great assistance to them in rebuilding their homes and in purchasing new flocks of sheep and cattle. But when Charles II came to the throne of England he declared that it was not his business to carry out the promises of his predecessor. So he seized the balance of that money for his own treasury.

In 1675 Charles Emmanuel II died, and his nine-year-old son, Victor Amadeus II, became duke of Savoy. While he was a youth, his mother actually ruled the country. As one of the new government's first acts, it confirmed the ancient rights and privileges of the Waldenses, guaranteeing them greater religious freedom than they had enjoyed for many years. The persecutions ended for a time.

The young duke had been in power only a year when a war broke out between Savoy and the people of Genoa. The Waldenses flocked to the banner of their prince and helped him win an important victory. The government expressed deep appreciation to them for their valor and devotion which helped win that war.

But in a neighboring country events were happening which would bring great sorrow to the Waldenses. In 1685, Louis XIV of France revoked the Edict of Nantes, which had given freedom to the Huguenots, as the French Protestants were called. The king declared that in the future only one religion, Catholicism, could be practiced in France. He commanded every citizen to join that church.

Many Huguenots obeyed the command and joined the Catholic Church though not actually believing what it taught. But others, who proved more faithful, went into hiding so they could continue practicing their Protestant religion. Many more, perhaps half a million, fled out of France, crossed the frontiers and began life again in the Protestant lands of Switzerland, Germany, Holland, and England. Some even fled across the Atlantic and settled in the American colonies.

Down near the southern border of France lay the country of the Waldenses. The king knew that some of his Huguenot subjects had fled into those valleys to live. He discussed the matter with his counselors, and they decided that all Protestants in the valleys should be forced to enter the Catholic Church or be driven out of their lands. A dispatch was sent to the French ambassador at the court in Turin.

This man approached the duke, Victor Amadeus, and informed him that the king of France, having rid his kingdom of all heretics, felt it his duty to see that the duke did the same to his lands.

This demand perplexed Victor Amadeus. He well knew the loyalty of the Waldenses; he could not forget their help in the recent war. He knew also that they would defend their religion with their lives. He hesitated to start a war on an innocent people who, when ruthlessly attacked, had so many times humbled the proudest captains of Savoy. But he also knew of Louis's tremendous power in Europe and of the great strength of his armies.

The duke ignored that first message from Louis, hoping that it would be forgotten. But the French king sent another message, urging in yet stronger language that the Waldenses be required to enter the Church of Rome. This time the duke sent back an answer which did not satisfy the French king. He only promised to investigate the matter and see what could be done.

For the third time the French ambassador appeared before the duke and delivered a still sharper message. His master, the most high and mighty king of France, had almost come to the end of his patience with Savoy. If the duke did not feel that he could cleanse his valleys of heretics, then the king of France would send an army and do it himself. If the king received no favorable reply from the duke, the French armies would immediately cross the frontier, reduce the Waldenses to submission, and then annex the valleys to France.

This last threat was enough for Victor Amadeus. The prospect of losing the valleys and having the French power established on his side of the Alps frightened him. He returned word to Louis XIV that he would carry out the wishes of the French king.

At the same time, Louis promised to help by providing a large army to cooperate with the duke's in this campaign.

One of the most powerful French armies moved up to the frontier, there to await word from the duke of Savoy that the time had come to march against the heretics.

13

A People in Exile

Snow lay deep in the Alpine valleys one fateful morning in January, 1686. Smoke rising from chimneys in many villages indicated that the families were keeping warm around their firesides. Suddenly the sound of a bugle broke the stillness of the winter solitude. Startled people, hurrying to their doors, saw a mounted soldier ride up to the meeting house, swing off his horse, and attach a long piece of paper to the door. Then, jumping into the saddle, he galloped off on his way to the next village.

The Waldenses knew that the man must be a messenger of the Savoy government. What notice could be sufficiently important to bring him into their villages at such a time? The men donned their overcoats and boots and went to the church door to read the paper, an edict issued by the duke of Savoy.

One of the village elders began reading aloud. The document consisted of nine paragraphs, each one like a spear, stabbing the hearts of the people. The first one simply stated: "The Waldenses shall henceforth and forever cease and discontinue all the exercises of their religion." A low moan escaped from the listeners. The man read on. They were forbidden to have religious meetings under pain of death and the confiscation of all their goods. All their ancient privileges were abolished. All the churches, prayer houses, and other buildings consecrated to the preaching of heresy would be destroyed. Every pastor and schoolmaster must become a Catholic within fifteen days or leave the country forever. All children must be brought up as Roman Catholics. All Protestant foreigners must become Catholics or leave the country within fifteen days. Those who refused would be permitted to sell their property to Catholic purchasers before leaving the country.

For several months the Waldenses had wondered why Piedmont soldiers had been gathering along the border of their country. They now began to suspect that these soldiers had been brought together to force them into submission to the edict of the duke. Word had also reached them that a large French army blocked the way out of the valleys to the west. How could they look into the future with any hope? How could they defend their homes against such powerful enemies? But how could they sell them and travel to new homes in midwinter?

All over the country the people gathered in their meetinghouses to discuss their troubles. The pastors urged them to keep calm and do nothing rash. Swift messengers on skis flew over the snowy mountains, carrying tidings of their danger to their fellow Protestants in Switzerland.

Another group of messengers went to Turin to protest to the duke, and to plead with him to suspend the edict. They pointed out to his officers that they had faithfully served in the recent war with Genoa. They reminded them of the peace treaty signed only recently by which they were assured that all their ancient rights and privileges would be respected. Would the prince not honor his promise?

To all of their pleadings the duke turned a deaf ear, refusing even to see the deputies. Perhaps he felt ashamed of his actions. But Louis XIV's threat to take the valleys hung over his head. He did, however, agree to postpone execution of the edict for a few weeks in order to give the Waldenses time to arrange for the sale of their property.

Meanwhile, roving bands from Piedmont, impatient to start the work of extermination, began to plunder and kill in the settlements nearest the plains. Likewise French soldiers now quartered at Pinerolo could hardly be restrained.

The news from the Waldensian valleys greatly troubled the Swiss Protestants. Several of their ablest men crossed the Alps to confer with the Vaudois. Other Swiss envoys went to Turin to protest and to try to persuade the duke not to carry out the dreadful edict. They were sent to the marquis de San Tommaso who was to answer for the duke.

At first San Tommaso insisted that the fault lay with the Vaudois who had taken up arms against their lawful ruler. But the Swiss envoys rejected his answer. Pressed for a true answer, San Tommaso finally admitted that pressure from France was the real reason for the edict. Taking the Swiss aside, he suggested they advise the Waldenses to submit to the edict. Let them go to mass, he said, and place their children under the instruction of Catholic priests for a time. As soon as they had satisfied the French king, the duke could quietly allow them to return unmolested to their own religious practices.

But the Swiss knew that the Waldenses would not agree to abandon their faith, even for a short time. Sadly their envoys returned and reported to the Vaudois the failure of their mission.

Representatives from all the valleys gathered in Chiasso on March 23, 1686, to discuss the situation. The Swiss pointed out the impossibility of resisting the well-trained armies of Savoy and France. "How could you fight against their cannons?" they asked.

"You are hemmed in on every side by the land of your enemies. There is no nation which can send you aid, because they cannot reach you. You do not have more than 3,000 fighting men to face 30,000 Piedmontese and French soldiers, some of whom are recognized as the best in Europe."

They went on to suggest that the Waldenses give up all thought of resistance, but leave their homeland and settle in Switzerland or among the Protestant states of Germany, where they could live in peace and preserve their ancient faith.

Perhaps the advice was good, but the Waldenses could not find it in their hearts to accept it. How could they bear to leave the mountains which had been their homes for eight hundred years? Besides, they would not be fighting alone. They remembered the many times in the past when a handful of their farmer-soldiers had defeated powerful armies of their enemies, They also remembered the great massacre twenty-five years before, and of how Cromwell, the powerful ruler of England, had stepped in and stopped the slaughter. They had been saved from extermination then. Could it not happen again?

Sadly the Swiss pointed out that conditions in England had changed. James II, a Roman Catholic, now ruled. Hence no help could be expected from that country. Every effort made by the Protestant powers of Europe during the previous twenty-five years to curb the power of the French king had failed. Louis XIV had four hundred thousand soldiers in his armies. What European nation could hope to challenge such a force or would even dare to do so in order to save a handful of people living in distant Alpine valleys?

The Waldenses left the meeting without having reached a definite conclusion. Some had fully determined to resist to the death the invading troops poised on the frontiers. Others believed the situation hopeless. They felt stunned by the magnitude of the danger threatening them.

One month after this meeting, the enemies advanced. The French army under the famous general Catinat, moved into the valley of San Martin while the soldiers of the duke entered the valley of Lucerna. They took some villages by surprise and killed hundreds of people. In other areas the Waldenses erected barricades and fought off the enemy for the time being.

Knowing from past experience that any campaign waged in the Waldensian natural strongholds would be long and bitter, the Piedmontese and French commanders wanted to try a different approach. Perhaps they might persuade the people to lay down their arms without fighting.

At San Germano, the French general announced to the people of that place that their brethren in the valley of Lucerna had laid down their arms and had been freely pardoned by the duke. Now they alone of all the valleys held out against the soldiers of their government, and he called on them to surrender.

The people of San Germano, positive that alone they could never withstand such foes, laid down their arms, and the French marched in. Instead of peace, a massacre of hundreds of men, women, and children followed. Those not killed or tortured were marched away into Piedmont to be distributed among the prisons in the towns on the plain. Some children were placed in monasteries and convents.

The armies subdued the valleys one by one in this fashion. Within a few weeks the land was emptied of its people. At last the valleys lay silent. No smoke rose from the cabin chimneys. The animals had all been killed or driven away. The goods of the people had been plundered. The churches had been desecrated and many of them totally destroyed.

Protestant Europe heard with horror of this new outrage against the Waldenses. Protests came from the German states in particular. The Swiss likewise sent another delegation to the duke of Savoy, urging that such an ancient people as the Vaudois should not be allowed to disappear from the earth.

Six months after the Waldenses had been herded into the Piedmontese prisons, the duke decided to yield to the requests of Protestant Europe and release those who still lived. But, he decided, they were not to return to their valleys. The people must go into exile, never to return.

Twelve thousand strong, liberty-loving mountaineers had entered the dark dungeons of their prince, For six months they had lived and died amid fearful conditions. Such food as they were given was often half rotten, and they did not have enough of that to keep them all alive. They had no beds on which to sleep, simply piles of rotting straw infested by thousands of insects and strewn on damp floors. They had no blankets. Summer passed into winter, and it became bitterly cold. Thousands died of hardships endured in those prisons. When the doors finally opened, of the 12,000 who had walked in, less than 3,000 crawled out.

The Waldenses' joy on being released was quickly dimmed when they learned that they could not return to their valley homes but must leave their land forever. Switzerland, they were told, would receive them, and perhaps they might go on to other countries in time.

"When must we go?" the Waldensian leaders asked.

"Immediately," the officials replied coldly.

The people shuddered at the prospect. It was late December, and deep snow already blocked the mountain passes. How could the women and children cross those mighty ramparts of snow and rock? Could not their exile be postponed until spring? They pleaded for permission to remain in the country for a few months.

Victor Amadeus refused the request. He did agree to provide the people with a little bread. Then, driven by their soldier guards, the helpless company walked out of Turin, heading northward toward the mountain passes. A storm broke over them as they climbed. Who can describe the horrors of that night? Helpless women and children stumbled in the snow and fell, never to rise again. The others struggled on and up, finally gaining the summit. There the guards left them to climb down the other side into the Swiss cantons. Those who finally reached Switzerland numbered only 2,600.

Word that the Waldenses were coming spread swiftly from one Swiss town to another. Kind-hearted people went out to meet them, carrying food and clothing. Their hearts melted as they saw the pitiful refugees walking, hobbling along the road, some with frostbitten hands and feet, mothers with babies in their arms or on their backs, so faint from hunger and weariness that they could scarcely stumble along. Their clothing, rotted in the long stay in Piedmont dungeons, hung in tatters from their bodies. The Swiss people offered them food, but many felt too faint to eat. The strong arms of the Swiss carried the children and aged persons to warm shelters.

Geneva in particular displayed a wonderful Christian spirit toward the exiles. Nearly half the city poured out to meet them, among them the aged Giavanello who had been exiled from the valleys by the terms of the peace treaty signed twenty-five years before. As he looked upon the pitiful remnants of his people, he lifted up his voice and wept. For some of the Waldenses, deliverance came too late. Some actually fell and died in the gateway to Geneva.

Swiss citizens made the refugees welcome in their towns. Many of the homes were still crowded with Huguenot refugees who had come pouring over the frontier from France just two years earlier. Nevertheless, they did not turn away one Vaudois who needed shelter and hospitality.

14

The Glorious Return

The people of Geneva could not adequately care for all the Waldenses who had come from Savoy. So the Waldenses spread through different communities of the Swiss cantons. Some had land, where once again they began to cultivate the soil and grow their own food.

Some of the German princes invited the Waldenses to settle in their territories. At the invitation of the elector of the Palatinate several hundred refugees entered his estate and settled among his subjects. Their hopes of finding permanent peace in Germany, however, were disappointed. Ever seeking new territory, the king of France sent his armies into the Palatinate. The inhabitants fled before the invaders. The Waldenses were among those forced to flee, so once more they took to the road in search of a place to live in peace.

But no matter where they went, or how kind the people, the exiles could not forget their native land. At twilight they would sit together recalling their ancient homes and speaking of the days when they had lived under the shadows of great mountains. They remembered how they tended their animals on the lush green grass of those valleys and watered them at the pure mountain streams. They spoke of the lovely groves of chestnuts which had provided food for themselves and their livestock.

Twice the Waldenses sent spies in disguise across the mountains to find out if any new people inhabited their valleys.

The spies returned to say that the people whom the duke had sent to live there had been unable to make the land produce and so had gone away. Fields lay untilled and grape vines unpruned. They heard only the sounds of nature. Hearing the spies' report, the Waldenses longed more than ever for their valleys.

"Better to die in our homeland than to live in exile," they said to one another.

Twice they sought prematurely to return to their valley homes, but each time the Swiss discovered and thwarted their plans. The authorities in the cantons kept a half-hearted watch over the exiles, knowing that should the Waldenses leave Switzerland and return to their native valleys, Louis XIV would certainly believe they had been aided by the Swiss.

But the Waldenses were not to be defeated. Fortunately they found a leader, Henri Arnaud, one of their pastors who had also served in the army of William of Orange of Holland. Arnaud secured financial backing from William, who was soon to become king of England, and with the support of some of the exiled Huguenots prepared another attempt to cross the Alps to the Waldensian valleys. In August, 1689, eight hundred Waldensian and Huguenot men gathered on the shores of Lake Leman. Arnaud had made all arrangements. Silently, under cover of darkness, the men stepped into boats and were rowed to the southern shore. This time, such of the Swiss authorities who knew of the escape did not stop them.

Fortresses defending the regular roads leading from Switzerland into Italy forced Arnaud to use the more dangerous mountain footpaths. From village to village they marched through the heart of the Alps, having no maps to show them which way to go, but watching the stars by night and pressing southward and eastward. They took most of these villages by surprise, carrying with them village officials or local monks as hostages, They also took some of the villagers to guide them from one settlement to the next.

Steadily the little company pressed on, always in great danger. Clouds settled over the mountain trails, and the men sometimes lost their way. Some days the rain came down in torrents. In the higher passes they even met snow and hail, the snow covering the ground up to their knees. Not until the eighth day did the Vaudois come in contact with enemy soldiers. By this time word had reached the defenders of the passes that a small band of Waldenses heading their way planned to invade the valleys.

News of this proposed invasion caused great merriment among the French and Piedmontese soldiers. How could a people who had been nearly destroyed three years before in the prisons of Piedmont, and then exiled from their homeland, expect to return and reconquer the valleys in the face of armies numbering more than 20,000 men?

When the Waldenses reached a narrow defile along the Dora River, they came to a bridge that had been built across the stream. Their scouts reported a force of 2,500 entrenched French soldiers prepared to stop their onward progress. Arnaud called his men together and discussed what could be done. Waiting until darkness had fallen, they advanced as silently as possible toward the bridge, prepared to risk everything in one tremendous fight.

The French sentinel, hearing mysterious sounds in the darkness, called out, "Who goes there?"

"Friends," replied the Waldenses.

But this did not deceive the sentinels, who immediately raised the cry, "Kill them! Kill them!"

The French army sprang into action. The mountain passes echoed with the roar of their infantry as a thousand guns went off. For fifteen minutes the French soldiers fired into the darkness. Arnaud had told his soldiers what to do when the firing began. Obediently they threw themselves flat on the ground and waited for the firing to stop. The bullets whistled over their heads but did no harm.

Determined to destroy these heretics, the French commander sent two companies of soldiers around to fall on them in the rear. For a moment it seemed that the Waldenses would have to yield. Arnaud saw their desperate situation. His men must conquer or die where they stood. To encourage them, one of his officers raised the cry, "Courage, the bridge is won!"

Actually, this was not correct, but the words had an electrical effect on the Vaudois soldiers. Springing to their feet they hurled themselves on the men guarding the bridge. They scattered the enemy soldiers, driving them from the field. Then they captured the heavy guns of the French before a single cannonball could be fired from them.

In the confusion of the night, the French commander received a dangerous wound in the thigh. Looking around in the darkness lighted by the flash of gunfire, he saw his fleeing soldiers. Reluctantly he ordered a general retreat. With a number of his officers, many of them dangerously wounded, he was carried to Briancon; but as he did not think his army safe even there, he went on the next day to Embrun.

"Can it be possible," he exclaimed, "that I have lost the battle and my honor as well?"

In the French camp the Waldenses found all the supplies they needed. They destroyed what food and ammunition they could not carry away.

The morning after the battle, the Vaudois counted 600 of the enemy dead on the field, while of their own number they had only fifteen killed and twelve wounded. Is it any wonder that Arnaud, their pastor-commander, led them in a great praise service to God who had helped them so mightily?

Their march forward continued. The day after the battle from the summit of the pass on Mont Sci they saw in the distance the peaks of the mountains which surrounded their beloved valleys. There on the mountain they held another religious service. The next day they entered a narrow defile where they found a company of Piedmontese soldiers prepared to keep them out of San Martin, one of their most beautiful valleys. No sooner did the Waldenses appear than a mysterious panic seized the soldiers in the pass. They fled without offering battle. And now, after an absence of three and a half years, the Waldenses once again stood upon their own land.

The next day they began to climb the Julien pass which would lead them down into the valley of Lucerna. As they neared the summit, a strong body of Piedmontese soldiers, posted behind barricades, confronted them.

"Come on, ye Barbets," shouted the soldiers when they saw the Waldenses toiling up the path. "We guard the pass, and there are 3,000 of us!"

The Waldenses needed no urging. Rushing forward they stormed the entrenchments and sent the soldiers fleeing down the other side of the mountains. In their enemies' camp they again found large stores of ammunition and food. Descending to the valley, they took possession of the town of Bobbio where they paused to rest for a few days. Then they continued their march until they reached Villaro, a town about half way between Bobbio and La Torre. They occupied Villaro but were unable to bold it when a large force of French soldiers overwhelmed them, forcing them to retreat to Bobbio.

Arnaud now divided his men into two bands. For several weeks they kept up a running fight with their enemies as they had done so often in the past. They would lie in ambush at points where they were least expected and then suddenly fall on the French and Piedmontese, put them to flight, and seize valuable supplies of food and ammunition.

Even though the Vaudois usually won in these skirmishes, they still lost men and their ranks grew thinner and thinner. When ten Piedmontese soldiers fell, replacements took their place. But when one Waldensian soldier fell, there was no one to take his place. Realizing that this type of warfare would surely result in the destruction of his entire force, Arnaud decided to mobilize them in some stronghold where they could defend themselves during the winter and wait to see what God had planned for them the following year.

He selected a natural fortress known as La Balsiglia in the upper end of the valley of San Martin. Here the mountains jutted out onto a platform washed by streams on two sides in the form of the letter V. This high position could not be attacked from the rear, as the mountain rose almost straight up behind the fortress. To this place Arnaud led his men, carrying with them what supplies they could collect.

At La Balsiglia the Waldenses cut down trees and built strong fortifications across every path or trail which might lead to their fortress. Having destroyed all roads and bridges for miles around, Arnaud now withdrew into this place with his 400 men, all that were left of that brave company he had led from Switzerland three months before.

Three days after completing the fort, Arnaud saw the forces of the French advancing up the valley. On the twenty-ninth of October, several thousand French soldiers marched forward to attack La Balsiglia from all sides. The French fought well, but they found the fortifications impregnable, and they were repulsed with great loss of life. Behind their strong walls the Waldenses beat off every attack without the loss of a man.

The first winter snow had already fallen, and the French commander realized that it would be impossible to capture the Waldensian position without heavy guns. These he did not have. He decided to retreat to a place where he and his army could shelter through the winter.

But before he deserted his camp in front of La Balsiglia, the French general sent the Waldenses a message. Under a flag of truce, an officer approached and was led to Arnaud.

"I have a message for you from our commander. He is leaving you now but will return next year at Eastertime. Then we will make an end of you, and you will have no escape."

"I shall be waiting here for your master," Arnaud replied.

The French officer bowed and left the fortress.

15

Defense of La Balsiglia

All the while the French and Piedmontese armies had fought against Arnaud and his little band of Waldenses they had tried to destroy or carry away all food supplies in the valleys. What animals they did not kill and eat, they drove down onto the plains. The Vaudois, moving from valley to valley, often hiding in eaves, suffered much from hunger. They passed many days with nothing to eat but roasted chestnuts.

Now isolated in La Balsiglia, the exiles looked out over the valley of San Martin and noted the utter desolation of the country. There was scarcely a cabin which had not been burned. They could not see a wisp of chimney smoke anywhere. Fields and forests alike lay beneath the white blanket of an early snow.

Arnaud realized that he and his 400 men in La Balsiglia faced a long, difficult winter. Choosing a band of his strongest and most daring men, he sent them over the mountain pass to the French valleys of Pragelas and Queyras. A few days later they returned bringing salt, butter, a hundred sheep, and a few oxen.

Then a miracle happened. A spell of warm weather followed the season's first snow. As the snow melted the Waldenses saw far below in the valley, fields of wheat which had not been harvested. Hidden by the protective blanket of snow, the grain had escaped the watchful eyes of the enemy. joyfully, the men left their fortress and harvested the food. Is it any wonder they felt that Heaven protected them? Morning and evening there in La Balsiglia, they raised their voices in song and prayer to God.

Some of those men in La Balsiglia had been born and reared in the valley of San Martin. One of them remembered a day more than three years before when the owner of the village mill, with the help of his friends, had hidden his millstone in the stream flowing around La Balsiglia.

"Better to hide it there than let the papists come and smash it," be had declared. The men in the fort now decided to make an attempt to recover that stone. Choosing some helpers, the guide led them to the spot. When they broke the ice, they found the millstone still lying there. Wading into the icy stream, they managed to get it up the bank. Then, pushing and shoving, they hauled it up the steep slope and into La Balsiglia where they set it to work grinding grain into flour for the hungry men.

But Arnaud still had troubles. He knew that the French army would return in the spring, stronger than ever. Unless God sent help, be and his little band had no possible escape. Yet as be reviewed the steps by which they had been guided back into their native valleys and the victories which God had enabled them to gain over large, well-equipped armies, he confidently told his men that the Lord who had led them thus far would not forsake them in the days to come.

As the winter days became shorter, the cold grew more intense. Between storms, the men left their fort to cut down trees from the nearby forest and work the timber into logs. They dragged these over the icy ground and up the slopes to La Balsiglia, where they piled them one on top of the other to form a strong barrier against any attacking army.

Winter ended and warm winds melted the snow. Foaming, singing water rushed down the streams. Over the passes from France came an army of 10,000 French soldiers.

Up the valley of the Clisone came 12,000 Piedmontese soldiers to join them, The Waldenses looked down from their fortress and saw the sun glitter on 22,000 bayonets!

Marshall de Catinat, one of the most renowned French generals of the time, commanded the combined army. He had many loaded wagons filled with food and ammunition. Hundreds of soldiers pushed and pulled strong cannons with which to batter down the fort of the heretics. Last but not least, Catinat had 400 ropes with which he intended to hang every one of the defenders of La Balsiglia.

"Fear them not," Arnaud urged his brave companions. "Remember, Gideon had only 300 men, so we have a hundred more than he did. Let us never forget what he was able to accomplish with the help of God."

Catinat carefully studied the fortress which he had come to capture. On one side a long slope led up to the fortress. He decided to use this for his army's approach. He did not know that Arnaud had fortified it with strongly built log palisades.

"One day," Catinat remarked to one of his officers, "should be sufficient for our army to overwhelm those poorly armed, hungry, unskilled mountaineers."

The French bugles blew early on the morning of May 1, 1690. The Waldenses watched fascinated as the first 500 men, flags and banners waving and led by Catinat on horseback, headed for the foot of La Balsiglia. The French raised a shout which echoed through the valley canyons. Behind that picked group of 500 came 7,000 crack musketeers who were to storm the fortress. With a tremendous shout they hurled themselves upon the palisade, but all in vain. Ceaseless fire burst from Waldensian guns, and the soldiers found it impossible to get past the massive tree trunks which barred their way.

When the enemy faltered, a band of Waldenses rushed from the fort, swords in hand, and under their fierce assaults from above, the French lines broke and the soldiers fled down into the valley. Very few of the 500 men which formed the first assault wave reached their camp safely. Of the Waldenses, not one had been killed or even wounded.

Catinat realized that he must make a new plan. Those great trunks must be destroyed. The only way to do that, he decided, was with his cannons. Across the ravine from La Balsiglia rose a piece of fairly level ground. Up onto this the soldiers hauled the cannons one by one. It took two weeks for the French general to get his cannons just where he wanted them. Then he felt ready for another attempt to conquer the Waldenses. This time he was sure he could not fail and that he would soon be able to put his ropes to work.

On the morning of May 14, 1690, the French gunners opened fire on the fortress. All day they poured a stream of cannonballs across the canyon against the ramparts of the fort. The mountains echoed with a sound never before heard in those solitary regions. By nightfall the once stout walls lay in ruins; there was nothing to prevent the enemy from marching straight up into the fortress.

Catinat determined that the Waldenses should not escape. He ordered great fires lighted that night all up and down the valleys. They illuminated the canyon walls so that the Vaudois could not steal away from the fortress and over the mountains without being seen.

The men in the dark, ruined fortress sent many prayers heavenward that night. God heard and answered them in His own way. About ten o'clock, sentries on the walls of the fort noticed for the first time that mists were beginning to gather around the nearby mountain peaks.

Word of this reached Arnaud and his men inside, and they came out to watch. Many times they had listened to the story of how centuries before, God had used a blanket of fog to shelter and protect their forefathers when threatened by destruction. Would this happen again? Eagerly they waited as the fleecy billows began to descend lower and yet lower down the mountain. The fog poured from cliff to cliff, and then in a few moments tumbled into the gorge of the San Martin River, sealing it in complete darkness. Looking out from the fortress, the Vaudois saw not a single fire.

But the question still remained—could they escape, and if so, where to? Behind them rose cliffs which no man could scale. Arnaud called his entire group together and asked if any knew the country well enough to try to guide them out. Captain Poulat, a native of the valley, spoke up. He knew a way over a razor-sharp escarpment leading past the enemy lines. Knowing that their only hope lay in getting away from La Balsiglia, Arnaud and his men placed their lives in the hands of this guide.

Noiselessly, marching single file, the men followed Poulat. In many places they had to move forward on hands and knees. In the gloomy fog they could see only a few feet ahead. Far below they heard the rush of waters as the river dashed over boulders and waterfalls. Years later, many of them came back to this spot to retrace the route of their escape that night. As they looked at the path they had followed, they shuddered, seeing that any man who tried to go over it even in daylight would be risking his life.

Down, down they went toward the river, shielded all the way by the friendly fog. Creeping past the French lines, they heard the soldiers laughing, singing, and boasting of the glorious victory they would win on the morrow. At the bottom of the gorge they crossed the stream and began to climb the mountain slope on the far side. The forest looked dark. Many times they stumbled and fell, but they spoke not a word as they climbed higher and even higher seeking a pass that would take them over and down into the next valley.

In the morning the rising sun burned away the mists. Catinat marshaled his army and ordered a grand assault all along the line. As the soldiers neared the ruined fortress, they raised a mighty shout of victory, expecting every minute to be assailed by men fighting for their lives. But they met no opposition. Scrambling over the ruins they swarmed into the deserted fort. They looked everywhere but beheld no enemy. Gazing around the mountains which rose on all sides of the valleys, a soldier suddenly pointed upwards. Far up near the summit they saw a small moving line of black dots. Their prey had escaped! The ropes would not be needed that day.

For three days the Waldenses marched, spending much of their time searching for food. When they reached Pra del Tor in the valley of Angrogna, they were surprised to find deputies awaiting them with an offer of peace from the duke of Savoy!

Victor Amadeus II had grown weary of taking orders from the king of France. William III, the king of England, had been urging him for some time to leave the side of Louis and join England, Holland, and the Austrian Empire and some of the German states in making war on the proud French king. As he was deciding to do this, the duke suddenly remembered that the Waldenses held many of the mountain passes. If he wished those gates to be closed and the French kept out, it would be wise for him to make peace with his mountain people.

In spite of all the evil the duke of Savoy had brought upon them, the Vaudois felt that he was still their rightful prince. They decided to accept his offer. Catinat now withdrew his forces to French territory.

Then Arnaud's 400 men returned over the mountains to bring back the remnants of their people. Only about half of the men who had so hopefully set out the previous summer returned to Switzerland. The rest had died in the struggle. Nevertheless, those who had survived joyfully led the remnant of the Waldenses across the Alps and into their native valleys. This time they marched along the main highways past those forts which had once threatened to destroy them. Back into their ruined valleys they went to begin again the heartbreaking task of rebuilding their shattered homes, replanting their orchards and farms, and restoring their churches. Generous gifts came from Holland, England, Germany, and especially from the Swiss among whom they had found a hospitable home during the years of their exile.

Once again the sound of singing rose from the valleys. Once again fathers, sitting near their cottages at twilight as the setting sun lighted up the glorious snow-covered peaks, called their children around them to repeat together those words of faith and confidence penned so long ago by the psalmist:

"God is our refuge and strength,
A very present help in trouble."

Seating himself, the stranger announced, "I am Victor Amadeus, your prince!" Durand, his host, was dumbfounded.

16

Tossed on the Waves of War

The Waldenses returned to their valleys in 1690 far poorer than they had been before persecution fell so fiercely upon them five years earlier. From 15,000 their numbers had been reduced to fewer than 3,000. Their homes and farms lay wasted. Some of their best pastors had perished in the dungeons of Turin. While thankful for the miraculous manner in which God had brought them back to their homes, yet they wept over their many friends and relatives who had died in the five-year struggle.

Once again the Protestant nations of Europe showed their concern for the brave Waldenses. From King William of England came a regular amount of money each year for pastors' salaries, a custom which the English government continued for more than a century. Holland likewise raised money for them as well as sending some dairy cattle. Universities in Switzerland willingly educated Waldensian students free.

In 1690 the duke of Savoy gave the Waldenses control of the fortress which had been built along the Alpine passes leading from France into Italy. He sought in every way possible to undo the great injury done to these people. He even restored all their ancient rights and privileges, including that of worshiping God as they chose.

Meanwhile the king of France was still persecuting his Huguenot subjects, who continued to flee by thousands from his country. The Waldenses welcomed these fugitives, whose skill and industry proved a great help in rebuilding the valleys. Among them came some of the finest pastors of the French Protestant churches. The valleys had twelve pastoral districts by 1692, and their religious services had been restored.

Many of the misfortunes of the Waldenses can be blamed on the geography of their country. Situated between France and Savoy, both strongly Catholic, the Waldensian valleys prospered when these two powers warred with one another and suffered when they allied.

In 1696 Victor Amadeus II once again joined the side of Louis XIV to whom he gave a promise that he would expel from his dominions all French Protestant fugitives. This meant that the brave Arnaud, who had led the glorious return six years before had to go into exile, for his birthplace was a valley on the French side of the Alps. The duke now ordered several thousand Huguenots, whom he had so recently welcomed, to leave their new homes within thirty days. With only those possessions they could carry, this band of exiles once more took to the road, seeking a place of refuge.

Passing through the thickly populated Swiss cantons, the Huguenots arrived in Germany, where they were welcomed and given places to live. Henri Arnaud went with them as their pastor and schoolmaster. William III invited them to come to England, promising to make Arnaud an officer in the royal army, but Arnaud declined.

In the valleys the old persecutions had again broken out. Children were kidnaped and carried into Catholic towns to be taught to deny the faith of their fathers and mothers. Heavy taxes burdened the Vaudois. Only the continued generosity of their Protestant friends in other parts of Europe enabled them to meet these obligations. Monasteries and convents were built at various places in the valleys. Priests and friars roamed everywhere, preaching the Catholic faith. Even the expense of maintaining Catholic institutions was laid on the Waldenses.

In 1703 war broke out again in Europe. Thinking that with the whole continent against Louis XIV, the French king would surely be defeated, Victor Amadeus switched sides again. The armies of England and Austria won many battles against the French in the north, but the French generals in the south defeated the duke of Savoy, even capturing Turin, his capital. They forced him to retreat with a small body of troops into the depths of the valleys where the persecuted but ever-loyal Vaudois lived.

One evening Penderell Durand, a farmer living in the valley of Lucerna heard a knock at the door of his cabin. When he opened it, he saw what appeared to be a poor, weary traveler with a heavy pack on his back.

"Come in! Come in, friend. Don't stand out there in the cold."

"Will you protect a poor wayfarer?" asked the man, looking around nervously.

"Of course," replied Durand, motioning his guest to a seat. He helped the man lay his heavy pack on the floor.

"I have no desire to offend you, but it is important that you answer one further question. Will you swear not to betray my presence in your home? I have need of rest, sleep, and food."

"A Vaudois never betrays a guest," replied Durand kindly, still puzzled as to who this visitor might be.

"I am Victor Amadeus, your prince!" replied the stranger to his dumbfounded host.

The Waldenses took good care of the duke, doing everything possible to make him comfortable. Before leaving two days later, Victor presented his host with a silver drinking cup, which the family always kept as a prized reminder of their royal visitor.

But the tide of war turned, bringing deliverance for the duke. When Prince Eugene of Austria swept into Italy with his victorious army, the Vaudois escorted their duke into the camp of that prince. Together the two men worked and fought until they drove the French out of Italy and saw peace once more restored in the valleys.

The duke of Savoy desired to help his Waldensian subjects, but he was not strong enough to resist the pope's demands that all heresy must be exterminated everywhere. The old petty persecutions, therefore, continued, and many new ones began. No Waldensian might become a doctor or a lawyer nor attend universities or other schools of higher learning. No Waldensian could enter government service. Monks and priests were as busy as ever, and the children continued to disappear.

Queen Anne of England and the king of Prussia both pleaded with the prince to cease mistreating their fellow Protestants. The duke sent a formal reply in which he promised to "preserve and protect the Vaudois and their children, and their posterity, in all their rights and privileges, as well as in regard to their abodes, trades, and the exercise of their religion to every other purpose."

This pledge helped for a little while. Then when Queen Anne died, the pope sent the duke a paper pointing out that he need not keep his promise on behalf of the Vaudois people. Because of this, the old troubles continued for another century.

Great changes occurred after the outbreak of the French Revolution in 1789. France ceased to be the protector and defender of the Catholic Church in Europe. No longer did she use her armies to crush her Protestant neighbors. The French government overthrew the Catholic Church in France, seized her property, and imprisoned thousands of priests, many of whom were killed.

The people tried the king of France and many of his princes and nobles as enemies of the state, executed them, and declared France a republic. Kings of other states in Europe became frightened lest their people follow the French example. In 1793, England, Austria, and Prussia declared war on France. The duke of Savoy joined them. It became very important that the passes leading from France into Piedmont through the Waldensian valleys be held to keep the French armies out of Italy.

Of all the forts guarding these passes, the most important was the strongly fortified watchtower of Mirabouc. Its strategically-placed guns guaranteed that no army, no matter how strong, could capture it, nor could any enemy pass by without being destroyed. When the French arrived at this pass and demanded the surrender of the fort, the cowardly Piedmontese commander decided to yield. Only one soldier in the fort protested, and he was the only Vaudois in the duke's service in that garrison. No one knows whether the French bribed the commander, or just why he acted as he did; but he surrendered the fort, and the French marched in.

The French allowed the Piedmontese garrison and its commander to return to Turin. There a court of investigation found the commander guilty of cowardice and condemned him to be shot. It noted the action of the Vaudois soldier and commended him highly for his effort to save the fort.

The people of Piedmont felt indignant at the surrender of the fortress. Since it lay at the head of one of the Vaudois valleys, someone spread a false report that its fall had been caused by Vaudois treachery. Suspicions flourished, and untrue rumors circulated which people would never have believed in time of peace.

Small groups of desperate men began to meet together and ask questions. Why should these heretics continue to practice their religion so freely and control the passes which they thus opened to the enemies of the country? The more they talked the more angry these men became. Fanatical leaders fanned the flames, and in the end they decided to massacre all Waldenses living in La Torre and the valley of Lucerna.

Before separating, these men agreed that everything should be kept absolutely secret, as they did not wish to involve the government of the duke. Seven hundred determined men joined this conspiracy, laid in a stock of arms, and planned the details of the coming massacre. They expected that the plot would be easy to carry out because practically all the Vaudois men were away with the armies on the frontier holding other passes against the French. They agreed that the signal for the massacre should be given at La Torre at midnight on May 15, 1793.

Word of this plot reached the ears of a Roman Catholic priest living in Lucerna. The idea of killing innocent women and children while the men fought for their country filled this priest with horror. He sought out Captain Odetti, the commanding officer in La Torre, and revealed to him every detail of the plot, including the date of the planned attack, Odetti was also a Catholic, but as a Christian man of honor, he likewise felt horrified. He determined to save the Waldenses of La Torre and the valley of Lucerna.

First he called the Waldensian women together and pointed out to them their great danger. He urged them not to leave their homes, particularly at night. Then he sent a message to the commander of the duke's army in which the Vaudois men fought, urging that a company of men be sent immediately to La Torre to prevent the massacre. The Protestant women of La Torre were urged to set up barricades, gather stones, and do everything they could to make their homes as strong as possible.

The first messenger arrived at the headquarters of General Godin, a brave Swiss officer in command of the Vaudois regiment.

"A mere panic!" he decided. "Because a few women and children have been frightened into fits by some phantom called up by the force of their own imaginations, they must needs have their fathers and husbands and brothers desert their post and conjure the ghost."

But the messenger refused to be dismissed lightly.

"As surely as you hold command of this army, so surely will the Protestant subjects of His Majesty fall victims to a plot unless you immediately interpose, or a direct miracle is wrought by heaven to prevent the catastrophe."

"Impossible!" exclaimed the general. "Human nature is not so utterly depraved."

"Ah, that is what people thought before the St. Bartholomew massacre in Paris," replied the messenger, more urgent than ever. I need not multiply instances. I only repeat that the danger is great and cannot be avoided unless by the strong arm of the government."

"When is this to be?" he asked the messenger.

"Tonight!"

"Alas, we may yet be too late," replied the commander, convinced at last of the truthfulness of the report.

Godin immediately sent for the officers of the Vaudois regiment serving under his command, and briefly outlined the dangers threatening their wives and children in La Torre. By hurrying they might cover the short distance to La Torre before the fatal hour of midnight.

These men did not need to be told to hurry. Along the road they ran, through the gorges, over the passes, clambering over rocks, wading the streams, never stopping for a moment. Even as they hastened, they sent prayers heavenward, calling upon God to save their families from the swords of their enemies.

The sun set behind the mountains, and darkness gathered in the valleys. The people of La Torre passed the hours before midnight in terror. About nine o'clock a great storm broke over the valleys. The rain came down in torrents. Soon the soldiers had to wade through streams above their knees. Brilliant flashes of lightning, while revealing momentarily the path they sought to follow, dazzled their eyes, then made even blacker the darkness which followed.

While the storm perhaps slowed down the march of the Vaudois soldiers, it did not stop them.

However, the violence of the elements terrified the would-be assassins. Many of them were waiting in nearby villages for the storm to cease.

It was nearly midnight when the Waldensian soldiers saw the distant lights of La Torre shining through the mist. Had they arrived too late? Then they met women of the town hastening toward them.

"Hurry, oh, hurry!" they urged the soldiers who needed no prodding. As fast as their weary feet could carry them, they pressed on toward those lights.

As they entered the gates of La Torre, they heard the bell of the convent begin to toll. The Waldenses dashed through the streets, prepared to strike down anyone seeking to enter their homes, but they saw no one.

The glad news, "They've come! They've come!" spread from house to house, as wives and children poured out into the street to welcome their deliverers. Plotters within the gates of La Torre witnessed the arrival of the Waldensian soldiers and wisely remained out of sight.

The next day, men, women, and children assembled in the Waldensian church to offer up praise to God who had saved them in the hour of danger.

17

The Last March First

For many years the tides of war continued to rise and fall around the frontiers of the Waldensian valleys. The French army under Napoleon succeeded in conquering nearly all of Italy. But two years later, when Napoleon took his army to Egypt, another group of great nations joined together to fight France. One of these nations, Russia, defeated a French army in Italy. The beaten French army, preparing to retreat across the Alps into their own land, found that they had 300 men so badly wounded that they could not possibly get them back to France. They left these men with the Waldenses of Bobbio.

Roistang, the kind Vaudois pastor of that town, brought out whatever he could to help the Frenchmen. From his own house he supplied a calf and twenty-five loaves of bread, while his wife tore up the family sheets and made bandages with which she bound up the wounds of the soldiers. Since only a few people lived in the valley, they did not have food for both strangers and Waldenses through the winter.

The pastor called his people together and discussed the problem with them.

"Never has a Vaudois refused to share his bread with a stranger, either friend or foe," he pointed out. "Yet can we take the bread of our children and give it to these Frenchmen?" he asked.

One old man stood up and holding out his withered hands toward his fellow townsmen spoke to them.

"Our prospects have been worse. Our fathers—under circumstances to which our own seem prosperous—had to fight many hard battles when their shelter was the cave, their foods the winter berry, the fallen chestnuts, or scattered ears of corn which they gathered from beneath a deep layer of snow. Yet all these—hunger, thirst, fatigue, cold, and continued watching—they endured with full and entire confidence that what they had undertaken as a commanded duty, the Supreme Director of events would enable them to support. An entire confidence in God casts out fear. Let us faithfully perform our duty as humble believers in His overruling providence and calmly wait the result. Let us 'remember them that are in bonds, as bound with them; and them which suffer adversity, as being ourselves also in the body.'"

The discussion continued. Some pointed out that by the middle of winter when no help could be expected from any direction, all food supplies would be exhausted and the soldiers and their hosts would together perish with hunger.

"I admit," said the pastor, "that it is our duty to minister to the wounded. But why not restore the entire detachment to their native country?"

"Restore them!" exclaimed the people. "But how? Without any means of transportation? Without horses, or mules, or wagons? Carry 300 men over high mountains, deep snow, imminent dangers?"

"True," resumed the pastor, "but we can restore them to their own frontier. Summon to the good cause the strength of our valley; employ every hand in the construction of litters; on these lay the sick and disabled, well protected from the cold, and our own fortitude will accomplish the rest.

"The pass," continued the pastor, "though terrible at this season to the timid, should never daunt us in so sacred a duty. Remember that the God who carried our people across the dreadful Alps and again brought them back, will still be the watchful guardian of His children. Resolve, my brethren! We have but one alternative—and on the manner in which we decide, the lives of many will this night depend."

A murmur of agreement went around. Then together they replied, "We are resolved!"

Everyone in the village now began to prepare for the fearful journey. They told their plans to the Frenchmen and then set about making litters. The French could not believe it possible for anyone to transport them across the mountains during that season when heavy snow lay in the passes. But as the Waldenses lifted them into the litters, they were moved to tears and called down the blessings of heaven on their friends, the Waldenses.

It was truly a fearful journey. They followed narrow paths, crossed foaming torrents, and passed beneath steep mountain slopes; they looked upward and prayed God to hold the snow in place and prevent the dreaded avalanche. At last they reached the summit and, passing through thick forests of fir, began the descent to the French side of the mountains.

Word of their coming quickly spread through the French valleys. Soon wives and children crowded around those whom they had long since given up as lost. The wounded French soldiers praised the Vaudois for all that they had done. Into their hands they pressed generous bundles of food to take back to their families. Then back over the mountain passes trudged the Vaudois, eager to return to their homes.

But sad to say, when the duke of Savoy heard of the incident, he chose to think the Vaudois were eager to help his enemies, the French. Because of their kind deed, he accused them of disloyalty.

Upon his return from Egypt, Napoleon became the ruler of France. With his army he crossed the Alps, defeated the Austrians and incorporated the Waldensian territory into France, making the Vaudois his subjects. Never had the people of the valleys enjoyed such peace and prosperity as they did during the years they were subjects of the French emperor. They worshiped as they pleased without restriction. Now Protestants and Catholics enjoyed exactly the same rights and privileges.

In 1805, Napoleon visited Turin. He received a group of delegates from the various departments of Northern Italy. Among them stood Peyrani, a Vaudois pastor as well as one of the moderators of his church. It is not known how Napoleon recognized the Protestant pastor, but stepping up to him he asked some questions.

"You are one of the Protestant clergy?"

"Yes, sir, and the moderator of the Vaudois church."

"You are schismatics from the Roman Church?"

"Not schismatics, I hope, but separatists from scruples of conscience, on grounds which we consider Scriptural."

"You have had some brave men amongst you; but your mountains are the best ramparts you have. Caesar found some trouble in passing your defiles with five legions. Is what I hear about Arnaud's glorious return correct?"

"Yes, sir, believing our people to have been assisted by Providence."

"How long have you formed an independent church?"

"Since the time of Claude, Bishop of Turin, about the year 820."

"What stipends (salary) have your clergy?"

"We cannot be said to have any fixed stipends at present."

Napoleon then asked whether they had not once received a stipend from England.

Peyrani admitted this was true, but explained that the Waldenses, now being citizens of France with whom England was at war, no longer received the money.

Napoleon suggested that the pastor draw up a memorial concerning the Waldensian church and forward it to him in Paris, Receiving this, the emperor arranged to have the Protestant pastors paid the same salary as that received by the Catholic clergy of his country.

Ten years later the empire of Napoleon lay in ruins. He had been exiled to the lonely island of St. Helena. But the Waldenses cherished his memory because of the freedom he had allowed them.

At the Congress of Vienna, which met after the fall of Napoleon, the great nations decided that the Waldenses should once more be restored to the kingdom of Piedmont. Remembering the affliction they had endured at the hands of former dukes of Savoy, the Vaudois felt uneasy about this decision.

In an effort to preserve the liberty they had enjoyed in the French empire, the Vaudois drew up a petition begging that there be no change in their religious rights. They even asked that a promise guaranteeing them this freedom be inserted in the new treaty. They placed this petition in the hands of the duke of Wellington. Unfortunately, nothing was done about it, and soon the Vaudois found themselves once more completely at the mercy of the duke of Savoy. Since the duke was violently anti-French, it is not surprising that he determined to show no favor to any former subjects of Napoleon.

Thus it came about that all their old troubles returned, now intensified. Priests swarmed through their valleys. Monasteries and convents were rebuilt. Children again disappeared, although the duke did make provision whereby parents would be allowed to see them provided they made no attempt to win them back from the Catholic religion.

Thirty years of intermittent persecution followed. Then in 1848, revolutions broke out in many parts of Europe. The duke of Savoy decided that the time had come to set his Protestant subjects free. On February 24 he issued an edict granting the Vaudois equal civil rights with all other subjects, and promising toleration in religious matters. The good news quickly reached the inhabitants of the valleys. The people crowded their churches, offering thanks to God for liberation from fear.

The proclamation concerning the Waldenses was only part of a new constitution which the king gave to all his subjects, granting them a larger share in the government. A grand parade was held on the Field of Mars in Turin, in which the Waldenses were invited to participate.

Six hundred Protestants from the valleys, headed by ten pastors, responded to the invitation. When they arrived on the parade ground, the spectators greeted them with shouts of "Long live our brethren from the valleys!"

The committee in charge decided that the Vaudois should march at the head of the parade.

"They have been last long enough!" they said. "For once at least, they shall be first." March at the head of the parade they did, and therefore were first to greet the king, Charles Albert, as he sat on a platform waiting to receive his subjects. Peace had come to the long-embattled Waldenses at last.

The Waldenses still live in their ancient valleys. Their ancestors fought alone for many centuries to keep alive the flame of gospel truth. Today their record shines as a monument of faithfulness despite danger, destruction, and even death; an inspiring example for all Christians who now carry the gospel torch, blazing the good news of salvation throughout the world.

We invite you to view the complete
selection of titles we publish at:

www.TEACHServices.com

Scan with your mobile
device to go directly
to our website.

Please write or email us your praises, reactions, or
thoughts about this or any other book we publish at:

TEACH Services, Inc.
P U B L I S H I N G
www.TEACHServices.com

P.O. Box 954
Ringgold, GA 30736

info@TEACHServices.com

TEACH Services, Inc., titles may be purchased in bulk for
educational, business, fund-raising, or sales promotional use.
For information, please e-mail:

BulkSales@TEACHServices.com

Finally, if you are interested in seeing
your own book in print, please contact us at

publishing@TEACHServices.com

We would be happy to review your manuscript for free.